Hamlet

WILLIAM SHAKESPEARE

Guide written by

Ron Simpson

A *Letts* EXPLORE Literature Guide

First published 1999
10 9 8 7 6

Letts Educational
The Chiswick Centre
414 Chiswick High Road
London W4 5TF
020 8996 3333

Text © Ron Simpson

Series editor Ron Simpson

Typeset by Jordan Publishing Design

Text design Jonathan Barnard

Cover and text illustrations Ivan Allen

Design © Letts Educational Ltd

Acknowledgements

The examination questions are reproduced by kind permission of The Northern Examination and Assessment Board.

Outline answers are solely the responsibility of the author, and are not supplied or approved by the Exam Board.

British Library Cataloguing in Publication Data

A CIP record for this book is available from the British Library

ISBN 1 85758 924 6

Printed and bound in Great Britain

Letts Educational is the trading name of Letts Educational Ltd, a division of Granada Learning Ltd. Part of the Granada plc.

Contents

■ Plot synopsis

The plot of *Hamlet* arises from events that have happened shortly before the play opens. Hamlet, King of Denmark, has been murdered by his brother, Claudius, who has not only seized the throne, but has also married his brother's widow, Gertrude. Young Hamlet, the late King's son, has returned from Wittenberg University too late to claim the throne, and he instinctively senses his uncle's evil.

As well as the family feuds, there is also a tradition of quarrels between Denmark and Norway. Thirty years earlier King Hamlet slew King Fortinbras of Norway and claimed territory from Norway as a result. As the play opens, young Fortinbras is preparing to attack Denmark to regain the territory his father lost.

Act 1 brings out all these plot lines, with the appearance of the Ghost of King Hamlet in Scene 1 contrasted with the smoothly political court of Claudius in Scene 2. By the time Horatio, Marcellus and Barnardo bring news of the Ghost to young Hamlet, it is already established that he despairs of the world and is consumed by hatred and disgust for his uncle. When he joins the others on the battlements in Scenes 4 and 5, the Ghost speaks to him and calls for revenge. Hamlet accepts the duty (deciding to pretend to be mad as a disguise) and the main plot is activated. Meanwhile, in Scene 3, Polonius, the King's chief counsellor, has seen his son, Laertes, off to France and has told his daughter, Ophelia, to reject all Hamlet's advances.

By the beginning of Act 2 enough time has passed for Polonius to decide to send a spy to Paris to watch his son, for the ambassadors sent to Norway in Act 1 to return successful and for Ophelia's rejection of Hamlet to start taking effect. From this stage until early in Act 4, however, the action proceeds almost continuously and, for the most part, in the same place: the halls, chambers and corridors of Elsinore Castle. Claudius and Polonius plot to find out what is wrong with Hamlet and, ultimately, to eliminate any threat to the throne. Hamlet seeks further confirmation of Claudius's crime and the opportunity and will to kill him. So Polonius, convinced that Hamlet is mad for love of Ophelia after he makes a dramatic appearance in her closet (private room – 2.1/2), forces her to talk with Hamlet while King and counsellor eavesdrop (3.1). The King sends for old school friends of Hamlet, Rosencrantz and Guildenstern, to discover the cause of his madness (2.2). Hamlet successfully resists these attempts to discover his secret (though Claudius realises that he is not really mad) and organises (2.2) a group of Players to perform a play before the King that will tell a story similar to his crime and strike his conscience. As a result of these machinations the play explodes into violent action in Act 3. The King reveals his guilt (3.2); Hamlet spurns an occasion to kill him at prayer (3.3); Hamlet visits his mother, kills Polonius eavesdropping and forces Gertrude to face up to her guilt (3.4); the Ghost reappears (3.4); the King sends Rosencrantz and Guildenstern to escort Hamlet to England, where he plans to have Hamlet killed (4.3).

In the brief pause from the main thrust of the plot in Act 4, Hamlet en route to England witnesses the passing of Fortinbras' troops on their way to Poland (4.4), but the most significant action concerns Polonius's children. Enough time has passed since Hamlet's departure for Polonius to be buried secretly and for Laertes to hear about it and return to challenge Claudius. On his return he finds his sister mad (4.5), and she later drowns, possibly a suicide. Claudius wins Laertes over and, as news comes of Hamlet's return, the two engage in a series of stratagems (4.7) designed to kill Hamlet in a supposedly friendly bout of fencing.

Act 5 focuses on two main events in each of which Hamlet and Laertes fight: Ophelia's funeral (5.1) where they struggle in her grave and the court scene (5.2) where the duel takes place. There is comic relief from the gravediggers and Osric, the foppish courtier, and Hamlet gives Horatio an account of his escape (5.2), a complicated tale involving pirates and the ultimate death of Rosencrantz and Guildenstern in England. However, the tragedy reaches its climax with the duel. Laertes and Claudius have planned three ways to make sure of killing Hamlet: unbated sword, i.e. with the point unprotected, poisoned sword-tip and poisoned drink. These three methods bring about four deaths: Hamlet and Laertes (from the poisoned sword), Gertrude (from the poisoned drink) and Claudius (appropriately, from all three). Hamlet forgives Laertes, begs Horatio to tell the story honestly to posterity and predicts Fortinbras will become King. Fortinbras now arrives and assumes control, and due ceremonies ensue.

■ The sources of *Hamlet*

As with many of Shakespeare's plays, there is dispute about the exact date of *Hamlet*: References to contemporary events in the text and by contemporary diarists to the play produce conflicting results (from mid-1599 to late 1601), but it certainly dates from approximately 1600. Therefore, the tragedy *Hamlet* which the pamphleteer Thomas Nashe wrote satirically about in 1589 was a different play. This so-called *Ur-Hamlet* ('Ur' meaning 'earliest') must be accounted a missing source for Shakespeare's play. It is thought probable that the play was written by Thomas Kyd, author of *The Spanish Tragedy*, an early and hugely popular revenge tragedy.

You will probably be familiar with the fact that, though original and innovative as a dramatist, Shakespeare was very happy to borrow plot outlines and transform them and even, in his earlier days, rewrite existing dramas. The interest in examining the sources is to detect the additions and transformations which Shakespeare made to sometimes fairly crude material. There are two main known sources for *Hamlet*, but unfortunately we can only guess which of the new elements originated with Shakespeare and which with the lost *Ur-Hamlet*.

The first source for *Hamlet* is Saxo Grammaticus, whose *Historiae Danicae*, published in 1514 but written over 200 years earlier, tells of Amleth. To summarise briefly, the brothers Horwendil and Feng (or Fengo) ruled Jutland under the King of Denmark. Feng killed Horwendil and married his wife Gerutha. Young Amleth, Horwendil's son, too young to avenge his father, feigned imbecility so that Feng took no action against him. Later, as Amleth grew to adulthood, Feng's suspicions of him grew. A beautiful woman was unsuccessfully employed by the King to seek out Amleth's secret, Amleth being assisted in defeating the plot by his foster-brother. A friend of Feng's spied on Amleth during a confidential talk with Gerutha, but Amleth killed him, chopped up his body and threw it into a sewer. Amleth then lectured Gerutha on her sins before confiding in her. Later, Fengo sent Amleth to England escorted by two retainers who had a letter asking the King to put him to death. Amleth changed the letter so that the escorts were to be put to death and he was to marry the King's daughter. It all worked out as he planned and he returned to Jutland in the middle of his own funeral service, killed Feng and became King.

In this you will find strong similarities to the outline of *Hamlet*. Important missing elements include the Ghost (the murder was openly done in the earlier story, so the message from beyond the grave was not needed) and a whole range of supporting characters. Perhaps even more importantly, both Amleth and the court belong to an earlier, less sophisticated society. Belleforest, who retold the story in his *Histoires Tragiques*, published in 1570, applied some element of sophistication in his moral commentary. Certain details of this second version are relevant to Shakespeare's development of the story. Feng incestuously seduced Gerutha before her husband's death in this version, and the beautiful woman who failed to discover Amleth's secret moved a step nearer to Ophelia by loving Amleth from childhood.

As well as the missing subplot of the Polonius family and other more minor narrative features, neither of these versions even begins to approach Shakespeare's insight into the mind and emotions of Hamlet. You will notice that the delay is dictated by purely practical considerations of age. The development of characters like Rosencrantz and Guildenstern or Horatio from rather anonymous beings who simply fulfilled a role in the plot seems to belong to Shakespeare, as does the schematic patterning of characters: the three avenging sons, Hamlet, Laertes and Fortinbras, for instance.

How much of the change could have occurred in the *Ur-Hamlet*? One would suspect very little of the subtle differentiation of character, but a contemporary account reveals that the author of the earlier play (Kyd?) can claim credit for introducing a ghost crying out for revenge and, presumably, therefore, making the murder a secret crime.

Other details come from various sources and there is no need for an account of them, but the case of Luigi Gonzaga in Urbino in 1538 is interesting. Gonzaga, a kinsman of the Duchess of Urbino, caused the Duke to be poisoned by a lotion in his ears. Given the name similarities to 'Gonzago' and 'Lucianus' in the play scene in *Hamlet*, it seems likely that Shakespeare derived Claudius's murder method from this historical source.

This variety of source material, so similar to and yet so different from *Hamlet*, makes its fusion into a dramatically, morally and intellectually satisfying whole seem all the more remarkable.

■ Texts and criticisms

If you are to achieve a high grade at A Level, some familiarity with the work of critics and commentators is desirable. However, such study has to be approached with care. The scholar writing on Shakespeare is not exempt from the opinions of his or her time and society, or of his or her political or moral stance. A critical work may be as much a reflection of the writer's Victorian morality or Marxism or feminism as of the play *Hamlet*. Also, the writer is usually aware of the variety of opinion already in existence and may therefore over-stress his or her viewpoint to counter existing argument.

There is thus a danger of reading one or two lengthy and challenging books and assuming that the views expressed in them are generally accepted as true. This may be more misleading than helpful. Furthermore, many of the most noted commentators on Shakespeare, such as J Dover Wilson, G L Kittredge and C J Sisson, expressed their view via prefaces and notes to editions of the text, so your starting point should probably be a good scholarly edition of the play. If you have not been issued with one, it is worth the expense of buying your own; there are several available in reasonably cheap paperback editions.

The editors of these editions are likely not just to present their own views, but to comment on those of other critics and to give a fairly comprehensive reading list, directing you to classic studies of *Hamlet*, like A C Bradley's *Shakespearean Tragedy* and J Dover Wilson's *What Happens in 'Hamlet'*. Without recommending a specific edition, we might note that the Oxford Shakespeare in World's Classics has nearly 150 pages of commentary, and the Arden Shakespeare over 300, both in addition to textual annotation. The widely available American edition by Bedford Books includes five complete critical essays. It is much wiser to make a good edition your starting point, rather than a persuasive commentator.

The text itself may prove something of a problem. Two editions of *Hamlet*, known as Quartos, were published in Shakespeare's lifetime, followed by the First Folio (a sort of 'Collected Shakespeare') in 1623. These differ considerably. So, too, do current editions and the text in performance: Hamlet is such a long play that few productions use an absolutely complete text. The Oxford Shakespeare is one edition that makes a case for omitting several well-known passages: they do appear in an appendix, however. This guide uses the Arden edition for quotations and line and scene references; depending on your text, you must be prepared for some adjustment.

■ Who's who in *Hamlet*

Hamlet

Hamlet

There are more plausible theories about the character of Hamlet than any other Shakespearean character, probably than any other character in drama and fiction. He has been sentimentalised into a romantic figure: Goethe described his as 'a lovely pure and most moral nature, without the strength of nerve which forms a hero' – an assessment which is not entirely acceptable, but contains germs of truth. Freud, on the other hand, and his disciple Ernest Jones, saw the basis of Hamlet's problems in the unnatural degree of his love for his mother, his Oedipus complex – again, difficult to accept as such, but an insight containing elements of truth. Hamlet assumes madness, but many commentators find real madness in his character. This, too, if not true in itself, draws attention to his unbalanced state. Speculation as to why he is delaying his revenge begins with Hamlet himself: he cannot explain it and wonders if he is a coward.

Bearing all this in mind, there is nothing wrong if you and your fellow students have different interpretations of Hamlet, so long as they can be supported by textual evidence. There is even debate on his age: according to Act 5, Scene 1, he is 30, but he seems much younger. How are we to say whether Shakespeare was being careless or whether he means us to find evidence of emotional immaturity or intellectual dedication in the eternal student of 30?

One source of accurate information on any Shakespearean hero is his soliloquies: traditionally they contain no lies or deception and express his own thoughts. What do Hamlet's tell us about him? The first (Act 1, Scene 2) reveals that the Prince is so melancholy that he does not wish to live, that he feels like this because of the death of his father and the remarriage of his mother (equally important), and that he views the world, notably womankind, with disgust. From this we can also deduce that he idealised his parents' marriage and that his acutely developed sense of honour and purity (especially in women) has been badly bruised. Later soliloquies confirm his distaste for life and humanity and intensify his contempt and hatred for Claudius, whom he abhors more as an unnatural being than as the person who stole the throne from him. Certainly the soliloquies tell us that the inability to act is a part of Hamlet's character, at least on this issue of revenge. Some critics claim that Hamlet has had no chance to kill Claudius, but he admits his inactivity in, for example, Act 2, Scene 2. Even in his attempted pep talks to himself, he retains the tendency to think around the problem.

Certain facts are clear enough about Hamlet. He is a considerable intellectual: his speech and interests express this and we should realise that, much as he loved his parents, university has been his chosen milieu until the moment when the Ghost bids him to seek revenge. He is suitably noble and pursues princely pastimes: his university studies have not diminished his skill with a rapier. His sense of honour extends to all forms of honesty, even to a hatred of affectation. This combines with an almost democratic tendency in his dealings with fellow students and gravediggers, but he can also assert the haughty authority of a prince.

Let us assume that his parents' marriage was very important to him. It is then possible to date his melancholy, his lack of emotional balance and his distaste for the world from the time of the murder and remarriage: these traits are not part of his previously established character. The time of the murder/remarriage is the point when his humour turned black and satirical, when he lost his delight in the world, when the cruelty entered his relationship with Ophelia. The noble prince who is recreated in various descriptions in the play, mainly by Ophelia, is different from, but not incompatible with, the melancholic who feels destroyed by the betrayal of others. His melancholy is not the fashionable emotion assumed at the time, but a genuine despair which no doubt limits his capacity for action. Ironically, the capacity for trust which seems dead in him surfaces from time to time, with tragic consequences in the duel with Laertes: his never-failing praise of Laertes suggests his basic generosity of character. With equal irony, the man who thinks too much to act is prompted, when he does act, by impulsive opportunism.

If you see more than one production of Hamlet, it is likely that the Prince will be interpreted differently in each. If you find this puzzling, it is worth reflecting that one of the most famed interpreters of the part a hundred years ago was Sarah Bernhardt, a French actress who played Hamlet for the first time at the age of 55!

The court

Although Hamlet is overwhelmingly the most complex character in the play, there are many other three-dimensional characters. In particular, the court characters are drawn in such a way that a convincing picture of court life and politics is created. Shakespeare's presentation of the court characters emerges as politically aware and surprisingly modern.

Claudius is a character distorted and corrupted by his own ambition, or sexual desire, or fraternal jealousy, or all three – whatever prompted his killing of his brother. Shakespeare is unconcerned about his primary motivation. He is a victim of his own guilt, yet we hear no one speak ill of him, except for Hamlet, father and son, and eventually Claudius himself (Act 3, Scene 3). He is described in consistently repellent terms by Hamlet, but we have no means of knowing whether 'the bloat king' or 'a satyr' are accurate comments. Shakespeare is most concerned with showing how Claudius operates as King and, in the early scenes, we can see how close to each other are the Renaissance Machiavellian and the modern 'spin-doctor'. (Machiavelli's *The Prince* was an extremely influential book of political theory. It inspired many Elizabethan and Jacobean playwrights to create characters noted for their ruthless political cunning.) Claudius is at pains to sanitise all his statements in keeping with the image he projects, to mount surveillance on potential enemies and to keep control of the words and actions (if possible even the thoughts) of all the court. He is an evil man, but an efficient monarch until guilt, Hamlet's plots and the death of Polonius drive him to ever more elaborate attempts to silence the Prince. These attempts end, of course, in silencing virtually the whole court.

Gertrude is often described by critics, on rather limited evidence, as a stupid woman, but she knows her role within the court procedures. There is a mystery about her: did she help with the murder? Probably not, but she is, to an extent, incriminated. She shared in the family life which Hamlet idealises: can she be happy with her present situation, burdened both with guilt and with Claudius? We cannot tell: she plays her role too well. Her life is based around concealment, projecting the caring empathetic side of royalty, until Hamlet confronts her with her sins in Act 3, Scene 4. As the court breaks down, Gertrude displays more and more affection and sadness: closely associated with the mad Ophelia, speaking the narration of her death, giving 'sweets to the sweet', regretting that Ophelia and Hamlet were not married, and finally meeting her death drinking Hamlet's health and applauding his success.

Polonius is the essential politician, knowing his fate to be linked to that of Claudius and making this his guiding principle. There are two problems with Polonius. Firstly, he can seem a harmless bumbler and is, without doubt, a highly amusing character. Surely, though, we know that shifty politicians can be laughably vain and fond of their own voices, and we must never underestimate Polonius's capacity for evil, even if he appears to love his children and has the endearing quality of forgetting what he is about to say. The second problem is working out what his role was in the Golden Age of Old Hamlet. He seems inextricably linked to Claudius (though obviously not to the extent of being involved in the murder of Old Hamlet), and yet he seems a career courtier/politician who has spent his life at Elsinore. There is no real answer to this, but we might remind ourselves of the 'loyalty' of senior Civil Servants to their Ministers.

To a notable extent these three main court characters speak publicly with one voice, and the same applies to **Rosencrantz and Guildenstern**. Taking the names of two sixteenth-century Danish ambassadors, Shakespeare creates characters who are a miracle of interchangeability (look at the King's and Queen's thanks to them in Act 2, Scene 2). Essentially, they have no characters: they are given a role at court which they accept unquestioningly. You will find traits of personality, like a taste for student-type jokes and a knowledge of theatre, but what they believe (if they believe anything) is unclear, beyond a desire to conform with the King's wishes and to be comfortable. Fate deals them a bad hand, but we cannot bring ourselves to regret it.

Other court characters reinforce the impression Shakespeare creates. Cornelius and Voltemand are barely allowed to speak, except in formal messages. Laertes, later an insurrectionist after the death of his father, originally seeks Royal permission to leave Denmark. The guards on the battlements represent the need for security, just as Osric represents the folly and foppery of the court, and for a time they, the Gentlemen and Officers, the celebrations and the firing cannon produce a false impression of the civilised, well-ordered court of a benign and legitimate monarch.

Ophelia

If Hamlet was over-sentimentalised in the nineteenth century, Ophelia suffered the same fate in more extreme form. Painters frequently turned to two scenes which are only narrated in the play (Hamlet's arrival in Ophelia's room in a state of disarray, and Ophelia's death) as the subject for paintings, and she was frequently regarded as an ideal of womanhood (or, more accurately, girlhood). Ophelia is undoubtedly the person who wished to marry Hamlet and whom he wished to marry. Her madness and death carry the intense pathos of the destruction of an innocent (and, we suppose, beautiful) young girl, a pathos increased by the refusals of the 'churlish priest' at her funeral. Beyond this we must be careful what we assume about Ophelia. There is no evidence that her rejection of Hamlet is a motivating force in his rejection of the world, let alone that it makes him mad. Each in a way rejects the other, she on Polonius's orders, he in Act 3, Scene 1. For the moment their love is somehow irrelevant to more pressing problems, but we do not know how things would have developed if Polonius had not been killed – Hamlet's obscene comments at the play suggest some sort of intimacy. Ophelia's appearances in the play are either rather neutral or extremely touching (madness/reaction to Hamlet's 'madness' in Act 3, Scene 1), but she, too, has been absorbed into the restrictive court atmosphere and, sadly, the hints of independence in her words to Laertes (Act 1, Scene 3) never translate into deeds.

Young men

Shakespeare uses a series of young men to contrast with, or complement, Hamlet. The most important of these, though not the only ones, are Laertes, Fortinbras and Horatio. The roles of all of them are defined by how they reflect on Hamlet.

Laertes is, in the beginning, very much the acceptable court image of a young nobleman – Claudius, one feels, would be much happier if Hamlet were more like Laertes, requesting permission to leave in polite and flattering terms, inheriting something of Polonius's talent for conventional platitudes. Laertes is always described as noble and honourable, not least by Hamlet, yet when he returns, his behaviour is anything but noble. Laertes is at least more positive than Hamlet as an avenger, but what does he achieve? It is difficult to believe that Shakespeare expected audiences to take Laertes as any kind of model for Hamlet's behaviour.

Fortinbras is different, in that we hardly see him in the play, he does nothing dishonourable and is widely accepted as Claudius's successor as King. Also, his activity in pursuing vengeance for his father at the beginning is certainly a telling contrast to Hamlet's comparative inertia. Fortinbras is a conventionally martial prince ('strong in arm', as his name says) and as such is a useful contrast to Hamlet, but he is not as opposed to him as some might suggest. After all, at the end Hamlet proposes him for King and Fortinbras praises the dead Hamlet.

The character of **Horatio** is developed from that of Amleth's foster-brother in the original Saxo Grammaticus story, the only friend of a hero surrounded by enemies. Essentially, Horatio's role remains the same. Not all the characters in Hamlet are the Prince's enemies, but no important character, even Ophelia or his mother, can be trusted by Hamlet. That, then, lies at the heart of Horatio's character: he is totally trustworthy and honest, not swayed by selfishness or emotion (see Hamlet's praise of him early in Act 3, Scene 2). His character is filled out effectively, with his sceptic philosophy, stoic courage and the speculations and easy humour of old college friends, but the essence of Horatio is to supply Hamlet with someone to trust and confide in – there are limits to how many soliloquies Hamlet can speak.

■ Themes and images in *Hamlet*

Revenge

Revenge

The revenge tragedy was a recognised type of drama in Elizabethan times. Although the play by Cyril Tourneur, entitled *The Revenger's Tragedy*, was published later than *Hamlet* (in 1607), Kyd's *The Spanish Tragedy* (1592), about the tragic revenge of Hieronimo, was a major success with late Elizabethan audiences. This climate of vengeance would have helped to clear the moral ground for Shakespeare's audiences to accept Hamlet's revenge as an honourable course. Although Hamlet has occasional doubts about the 'honesty' of the Ghost, both he and audience are convinced of the evil of Claudius – Hamlet is convinced even before the Ghost appears. It is his duty as a son, even more so after he has administered the test of the play scene, to avenge his father.

Shakespeare's subtlety of treatment of the theme of revenge depends on various developments. Obviously, the character of Hamlet is that of an unlikely avenger, so the play is largely occupied with uncertainties, delays and counter-plots, not the actual prompting to revenge: the Ghost's message is clear and occurs early in the play. It thus becomes a more internal quest for revenge: moral questionings and self-lacerating analyses of character take centre stage. A further development, of course, is a pattern of avengers. Three young men feel that their fathers need to be avenged, though Fortinbras' father has not been murdered like Hamlet's or Laertes'. Elsewhere (including in the **Who's who** section) the effect of these secondary avengers is discussed.

Corruption

Corruption

For Hamlet, the thrust for revenge is, in part, a need to put things right. The world is corrupt, much of the corruption spreading out from the incestuous marriage of Claudius and Gertrude. The images of corruption, decay and rottenness dominate the play. Many of these come from Hamlet's diseased sensibility, but by no means all. 'Something is rotten in the state of Denmark', says the relatively down-to-earth Marcellus without even knowing what the Ghost has to say. The madness and death of Ophelia is related to the withering of flowers (for instance, 'they withered all when my father died'). The Ghost speaks of 'leperous distilment' and 'vile and loathsome crust'. For Hamlet, though, corruption in its various forms is seldom out of his mind: Claudius is 'a mildew'd ear' (of corn); the marriage is an 'ulcerous place' concealing 'rank corruption'; Gertrude continuing in the marriage bed is spreading 'compost on the weeds/To make them ranker'; the world is 'an unweeded garden' possessed by 'things rank [a favourite word] and gross in nature'; Hamlet dwells upon the decay of the human body in Act 4, Scene 3 ('we fat ourselves for maggots') as well as in the graveyard. These few examples merely sample the recurring imagery – you can find many more.

Linked with the images of corruption is opposing imagery, including images of god-like honour for Old Hamlet and of fresh flowers for Ophelia. Variations on the corruption imagery are Hamlet's disgust at the 'frailty' of women and the concept of 'the world turned upside down', things being opposite to what they should, well shown in Hamlet's comment that it is not surprising that children have taken over the theatre, 'for my uncle is King of Denmark'.

Madness

Madness

One of the most memorable features of *Hamlet* is the presentation of madness, but perhaps it is less central to the play than some commentators suggest. The debate on whether Hamlet is mad is sterile. Clearly he is not, though equally clearly his mind and emotions are troubled and less than 'wholesome', to use the Shakespearean word. In Act 1, Scene 2, this noble, well-bred prince cannot manage a civil word to his step-father and thinks he would rather be dead (not that he plans to do anything about it). He then talks to his old friend, Horatio, with bitter irony followed by incisive clarity once the Ghost is mentioned. On the battlements, philosophising is followed by reckless courage, wild excitement, semi-comic exchanges with an unseen ghost and a warning that he is to assume madness. This behaviour in the opening act explains perfectly well all his future conduct. With the possible exception of the visit to Ophelia (to out-fox Polonius or simply an expression of his disgust at women?) his 'mad' scenes have a purpose: to confuse or frighten Claudius, to put Polonius or Rosencrantz and Guildenstern off the scent, etc. If he indulges in some malicious humour as well, that is understandable. Between times he acts sanely, with occasional 'wild and whirling' outbursts which stop well short of insanity.

Then there is Ophelia's mad scene. Madness was a more common feature in Elizabethan drama than it is today: the idea that 'a young maid's wits' were perilously mortal would have struck a chord with theatre audiences. Despite the conventional 'mad songs', this scene avoids many of the less convincing features of such scenes: Ophelia's madness has its tragic consequence (there is no sliding in and out of madness) and the madness is thoroughly integrated into plot and theme. Ophelia's madness and Hamlet's 'madness' provide a contrast in perceived types: Ophelia's madness is simply a loss of wits, inspiring pity and pathos, whereas Hamlet's presents an aggressive and dangerous distortion of the world.

The family

The family

This is a family tragedy at the same time as one of Shakespeare's most intensely political plays. Two families are at the centre of events: the Royal Family and the family of the King's chief adviser. The Royal Family appears to be secure from opposition within the country until the members embark on their own internecine warfare. Laertes only raises the people briefly in revolt after the King and his nephew have commenced their bloody feud. The threat from Norway is dealt with efficiently by war (Old Hamlet) or diplomacy (Claudius), and Fortinbras assumes the Danish throne by consent when all members of the Royal Family are dead.

Therefore, compared with many royal houses in Shakespeare's plays, that of Denmark is secure, except from itself. The play's scale is far more than domestic, but the family is at the heart of it. Note that Hamlet's first two lines stress 'kin' and 'sun/son', and Claudius's early concern is that Hamlet should regard himself as his son, an idea later mocked by Hamlet in 'uncle-father and aunt-mother' and in calling Claudius his mother before leaving for England. The bitterest expression of the family relationship comes in Act 3, Scene 4, when Hamlet describes Gertrude as 'your husband's brother's wife' and wishes she were not his mother. The family relationship of Hamlet's parents and himself is idealised by Hamlet, and his disgust at womankind stems form the sexual debasement of his mother in what he sees as incest. (Marriage with a deceased husband's brother was regarded technically as incest, though there is, of course, no blood relationship.) Hamlet's revenge is family-related at least as much as it is power-related. The first statement of Claudius's murder reveals this family/power connection neatly: the Ghost refers to the serpent who 'wears his *Crown*' and Hamlet follows up with 'my *uncle*'.

It is interesting that the other main political figure, Polonius, is presented in a family setting. His first appearance is to agree unwillingly to his son's departure, and this is followed by an extended scene with his son and daughter. He maintains remote control of his son and uses his daughter as a political weapon. When he is killed, the consequences for the Royal Family come via his family, not some political faction.

Even the dramatic inserts dwell on family: the victims of 'the hellish Pyrrhus' are 'fathers, mothers, daughters, sons' and finally, 'old grandsire Priam', while the Player King and Queen engage in a long debate on the sanctity of marriage.

Humour

Hamlet contains more humour than any other Shakespearean tragedy, without diminishing the power of the tragic plot. This is due to the type of humour deployed. The only clown scene features two gravediggers – very droll, but very macabre. Hamlet himself is talented at wordplay and satire: his melancholy does not diminish this, but directs it in a sardonic vein of black humour. Hamlet's intelligence (together with a certain aristocratic disdain) does not allow him to suffer fools gladly, but Shakespeare has the acute insight that fools can also be dangerous: we enjoy his mockery of Polonius and Rosencrantz and Guildenstern while realising that it is also a defence against men whose stratagems might help to bring about his death. In the same way the comedy of their characters (the lack of individuality of Hamlet's college 'friends' or the fussy preoccupation with control and deception of Polonius) are in keeping with their roles as part of Claudius's political machine.

Guilt

Claudius is guilty of killing Old Hamlet in circumstances which give no opportunity for atoning for his sins: 'cut off even in the blossoms of my sin', Old Hamlet's spirit has to expiate his guilt in Purgatory. The presentation of guilt is, obviously, central to the play. There are, however, some aspects of this presentation that are less obvious. Note, for instance, the fact that the nearest we come to sympathy for Claudius is in Act 3, Scene 3, where he confesses his guilt, but compounds it by admitting that his remorse is not sufficient for him to atone by giving up what he has gained by evil.

The question of Gertrude's guilt is often broached. Hamlet says, 'To kill a king and marry with his brother', but there is no suggestion elsewhere in Hamlet's heart-wringings or her own words to support the idea that she was involved in the murder, and it is reasonable to think that Hamlet sees both sins as one act. How much does Gertrude know and since when? This is more debatable, but her sense of guilt seems to be for her 'o'er-hasty marriage' rather than anything worse.

Hamlet, of course, shares in the sense of guilt in the play, and not just for failing for so long to fulfil his duty to his father. In Act 3, Scene 1, he says to Ophelia, 'I could accuse me of such things that it were better my mother had not borne me.' Like so much that he says, this is part of his 'antic disposition', but contains a hint of his actual views. The guilt that Hamlet feels, as expressed in this speech, is part of his current contempt for mankind: 'arrant knaves all'.

Examiner's tips

Examination

Coursework

These icons are used throughout the **Text commentary** to highlight key points in the text, provide advice on avoiding common errors and offer useful hints on thoroughly preparing yourself for coursework and examination essays on this play. They mark passages of particular relevance to the sections on **How to write and examination essay** and **How to write a coursework essay**.

Text commentary

Act 1, Scene 1

The first appearance of the Ghost of Hamlet's father.

Exposition

The exposition of a play or novel is the section, usually at the very beginning, where the state of the plot and characters is explained so that the ensuing action makes sense to the audience or reader. In relation to Shakespearean tragedy, Bradley defines it as the part which 'sets forth or expounds the situation, or state of affairs, out of which the conflict arises'. Exposition can be either *direct* (where we are simply told what the situation is, as in plays that use a Chorus) or *indirect* (where conversation or reaction reveals the existing situation).

In Act 1, Scene 1 of *Hamlet*, Shakespeare, as he often does, chooses to begin with minor characters (Horatio is somewhat more than minor, but the others appear only in the first act), so that the protagonist and other leading characters can be placed in a setting that the audience already, in part, understands.

Let us examine what we learn in this scene and how we learn it by indirect exposition. The play begins with nervous exchanges between sentries on castle battlements. This creates atmosphere, of course, but what does it reveal?

The relationship between Denmark and Norway provides crucial background to the play. Historical conflict between the countries and their kings (often called simply 'Denmark' and 'Norway') and current uncertainty provide impetus to the plot, insight into characters and a point of comparison for Hamlet. We learn about these relationships here through Horatio: how does this information occur naturally in conversation?

The appearance of the Ghost after only 42 lines gives the play a highly dramatic start. How is the Ghost's appearance prepared for? Though the Ghost's message is for Hamlet alone, its appearance reveals the death of the late King, hints at something amiss in his death and provides the opportunity for further exposition.

Finally, note that the closing lines lead directly into informing 'young Hamlet' and the certainty that the Ghost will speak to him.

Horatio and the Ghost

Horatio is, in many ways, an inspired creation, providing insight into Hamlet the university intellectual, and offering an alternative, stoic approach to suffering. He is the sounding board for Hamlet's plots and the guardian of his reputation after death. Here, he has a specific role. He is a philosopher, a sceptic, and therefore does not believe in ghosts and such superstitions: 'Tush,

tush, 'twill not appear', he says at first (line 33), and even late in the scene he says, of the legend that evil spirits do not appear at Christmas, 'So have I heard and do *in part* believe it.' Yet this man accepts the Ghost at face value: how can we do otherwise?

The question that Hamlet later has to confront is whether it is 'an honest ghost' (1, 5, line 144). In other words, 'Is it genuine and truthful or an evil spirit?'. In this first appearance, the Ghost inspires fear even before its entry: check how it is described in the dialogue. Horatio's first question implies that it may not be 'honest', asking what it is that usurps the form of the King of Denmark. The word 'usurp' means to claim without right: who in the play has really usurped the form of the King of Denmark? The disappearance at cock-crow suggests that it is an evil spirit.

However, no reader or listener sensitive to language can really believe that the Ghost is evil. By the end of the scene, though still referring to the Ghost as 'it', Horatio and the others clearly recognise it as the troubled spirit of Hamlet's father. Horatio's speech (from line 130), with its repeated use of 'speak', gives possible reasons why the King should wish to return. Marcellus (line 148) is concerned that they should respect so 'majestical' (literally 'kingly') a being. It is a *revenant* from the grave, a ghost with a secret, and debate on whether it is in Purgatory or not is unhelpful dramatically. Later, in Act 3, the Ghost *may* be seen as a product of Hamlet's conscience, but not here.

Examiner's tip

The attitude to the Ghost of the sceptical Horatio and his companions is important in establishing the basis for Hamlet's quest for revenge (as in question 1, page 73). They discuss its possible nature, but there is a basic conviction that it is to be respected, that it brings a message and that Hamlet must be told.

Examination

The Ghost's mission is understood by the sentries. Horatio says, 'This bodes some strange eruption to our state' (line 72) and, in lines which do not appear in all editions, Barnardo calls it 'portentous' (in other words, serving as a portent or omen) and Horatio tells a story of Roman times and omens of the death of Caesar. This form of partial exposition (the Ghost has a message, but what is it?) leads to surmise and suspense at the very start of the play.

Is something rotten in the state of Denmark? Marcellus's famous line will not be delivered for another three scenes, but you may already have picked up hints that all is not well in Denmark. Examine this first scene for indications of possible 'rottenness'. You will find general suggestions, but probably very little that is in any way precise: is there any indication, for instance, of Claudius's evil? You may also look at the moods created by descriptions:

Corruption

of night on the battlements or the comparison to Imperial Rome. The final descriptions, of 'wholesome' nights and the coming of dawn, offer relief and contrast after the terrors of the night. The scene ends in tension and expectation, with Horatio and Marcellus driving us into the next scene with their determination to tell Hamlet about the Ghost.

Act 1, Scene 2

The first court scene, with signs of conflict between Claudius and Hamlet, and Horatio's news of the Ghost.

Claudius holds court

For 128 lines Claudius dictates the form of the scene, except for Hamlet's brief

asides and explosion on the word 'seems'. He delivers formal speeches, he tells the ambassadors what to do, he invites Laertes to petition him, he asks Polonius his views and he even launches into a moral homily on Hamlet's need to see him as a father. It is a wonderful demonstration of the power of 'seeming': he is, in the modern term, his own spin-doctor.

The court

Notice that all except Hamlet know how to please the King – they make copious use of terms like 'duty', 'dread lord' and 'gracious', they frame requests as humble pleas with words like 'beseech' and 'leave and pardon'.

Let us examine Claudius's first speech to see how his character is brought out by the diction, imagery and syntax. He has one piece of news to impart:

he is sending ambassadors to the King of Norway to persuade young Fortinbras to call off his demands for land. This is cloaked in terms that attempt to establish his legitimacy as King and to gain the unanimous support of the court.

The court

The opening sentences are full of subordinate clauses that suggest reasoned conduct: 'Though yet…, yet so far… that… Therefore…'. The speech glows with a polish that suggests thorough preparation. Even his grief and happiness are formally balanced, with a series of beautifully poised oxymorons: 'a defeated joy… an auspicious and a dropping eye… mirth in funeral… dirge in marriage' (lines 10–12). He hints at the co-operation of the court in a general way: their 'better wisdoms' have gone 'freely' along with this 'affair'. What 'affair' is this? How has the court supported Claudius? What does this suggest of their relationship?

The court

At the outset of the play Claudius appears to be safe in power. This is therefore one of the best scenes to demonstrate the complete control he exercises over his court. When writing about **Coursework** this do not simply deal with his attempts to control Hamlet – look at his language and behaviour towards the entire court.

Shakespeare brings out perfectly the mixture of smooth flattery, vanity and ruthlessness in Claudius. He twice takes the opportunity to pay tribute to his brother (as though the transfer of the Crown had not involved murder) and reminds us of his position as King with painfully frequent use of 'we', 'us' and 'our'. The steel beneath the charm emerges in dismissive comments about Fortinbras ('So much for him') and his instructions to Cornelius and Voltemand: do not step outside your orders! This is centralised government in the hands of a shrewd politician.

Examine the exchanges between Claudius, Laertes and Polonius to discover how language is used to promote the King's image of himself and to seal the loyalty of Laertes and Polonius.

Hamlet revealed

It is fitting that such a complex character as Hamlet should be revealed in such a variety of situations in his first appearance. A key part of the exposition is that which tells us about Hamlet's character and situation, and he is shown here from many different angles.

In the formal court scene his disgust for his uncle means that he virtually refuses to speak to him. He makes two bitter puns about kinship, the first one of which may be delivered as an aside, and that is the limit of his conversation with the King. He is 'less than kind' in the sense that, though related, he is totally lacking in family feeling for Claudius; he is 'too much in the sun' because he rejects Claudius's claims of a father/son relationship. Otherwise he speaks only to his mother, most pointedly (line 120) when he agrees not to go to Wittenberg, a remark which Claudius pretends is 'a loving and a fair reply'.

The family

The qualities of Hamlet revealed in this first section are his fervent hatred of pretence, his devotion to his father's memory and his instinctive awareness of Claudius's evil. How has Hamlet been behaving since his father's death? Of what exactly do you think he suspects Claudius?

Hamlet's character and role are established more through soliloquy than those of any other Shakespearean tragic hero. Much of the drama is internal, within Hamlet. Notably given to self-analysis, and plagued by melancholy and disgust at the world, he finds the prospect of suicide tempting throughout the first half of the play. Compare the soliloquy (lines 129–159) with 'To be or not to be' in Act 3, Scene 1, and examine the different reasons he cites for not committing suicide.

Traditionally, soliloquies always reveal the true feelings of the speaker, and in this case his melancholy and disgust are based on one event only. To begin with he expresses his emotions in general terms. His flesh is 'sullied' (usually the preferred reading to 'solid' for modern editors), the world is 'an unweeded garden', taken over by 'things rank and gross' (two very typical adjectives for Hamlet). Why does the whole world seem like this to him? Not because his father is dead or he suspects Claudius of murder, but simply because his mother has betrayed the ideal relationship of his parents by an instant and incestuous marriage.

Corruption

Examine the way Hamlet presents his feelings about the Old Hamlet/Gertrude/Claudius triangle in lines 138–158: find examples of the use of broken sentences to convey intensity of emotion; note the different terms in which he speaks of the two marriages, including Classical comparisons (Hyperion was the beautiful sun-god, satyrs were deformed half-man, half-beast creatures); think about how Hamlet generalises about women from one example and what this will do to his relationship with Ophelia.

Even in this first scene the many facets of Hamlet's character are well revealed. From the surly opponent of majesty and the melancholic who can see no good in humanity, he emerges as the good companion of university days and an efficient and soldierly questioner and planner.

'But break, my heart, for I must hold my tongue' introduces the arrival of Horatio and the sentries. What does it mean? Does he not want to upset his mother by speaking the truth? Is he afraid these newcomers will overhear him? Or is this a court where nothing but the party line is allowed – unless, of course, you are mad?

A C Bradley, whose approach to Shakespeare is very character-based, begins his analysis of Hamlet's character by trying to work out what Hamlet was like 'just before his father's death'. In the final section of this scene there are hints of the pre-trauma prince. The sense of humour and casual student banter may be darkened by disgust at Danish drunkenness and too hasty a marriage, but they can still be perceived. More important,

Hamlet

notice the acceleration that occurs after Horatio's narrative. Hamlet has listened patiently, but now the interrogation begins: quick-fire questions are followed by a decisive, 'I will watch tonight' and exact instructions to the others. This Hamlet is not merely an inactive and melancholy poet.

Act 1, Scene 3

Laertes' departure and two lectures for Ophelia.

The Polonius sub-plot

The use of Polonius's family to provide a sub-plot to Hamlet's activities is managed with great subtlety. They take part in some scenes that have no bearing on Hamlet (notably the first part of Act 2, Scene 1) and appear as a recognisable family unit in their own right, as in this scene. However, the interlocking of their affairs with Hamlet's means that the sub-plot constantly feeds the main plot with incidents and parallels. Already, by the end of this scene, Polonius has been revealed as the representative of the politically correct court and has taken a major step in the dangerous isolation of Hamlet: he has ordered Ophelia to end her relationship with Hamlet, which will combine with Hamlet's already held views on the frailty of women. Laertes is already seen as some kind of a parallel to Hamlet: in Scene 2 his request to depart, framed in very different style to Hamlet's, was granted and the Prince's rejected. The parallel will become much closer until each proves the other's nemesis. As for Ophelia, her connection to the main plot is clear from the moment Laertes starts to lecture her on Hamlet's 'favour'.

The family

This scene is an excellent example of how Shakespeare is able to present serious material in an amusing way. Even the organisation of the scene is amusing: three sections of very similar length, each consisting of a lecture to an unresisting, but possibly unconvinced, listener. Laertes has early learnt from his father how to deliver a pompous and prolix speech and Ophelia's response gently deflates his dignity. Laertes seeks to escape ('I stay too long') before Polonius enters, reproves Laertes for being late departing and delays his departure further by more than 20 lines of 'precepts'. The humour of the situation reversed (lecturer becomes lectured) is then overtaken by the significance of the final section between Polonius and Ophelia.

How seriously do we take Polonius?

Laertes' speech is formal and cautious, full of 'thens' and 'therefores' and conditional statements, with much use of 'may' and statements like 'It fits your wisdom so far to believe it...'. It is a very middle-aged speech and the appearance of Polonius suggests that Shakespeare intends us to find a family resemblance. Polonius's speech to Laertes sounds prepared, with 'precepts' applicable to almost any situation.

The court

Not only literary critics, but also producers of the play have a decision to make on whether Shakespeare is presenting Polonius as wise or comic here. In making up your mind, consider the following questions: Are the individual precepts good advice? Does Polonius really believe them: 'to thine own self be true', for instance? Why is he delivering them at this point? Why does Laertes respond with no more than a farewell?

Polonius is much more aggressive in tone with Ophelia. Compare the smooth and balanced verse of 'Give every man thy ear, but few thy voice' with the broken lines, questions and demands like 'Give me the truth' that characterise the later scene. Here, he is emotionally committed and a simile such as 'like sanctified and pious bawds' shows little concern for his daughter's delicacy. Yet even here he cannot resist a play on words, with the various meanings of 'tender'. Polonius is a dangerous schemer, a co-conspirator with an evil king, a dominating father and sometimes a wise politician, but he never entirely escapes the comic role of 'tedious old fool'.

Tragedy

If you are examining whether comedy tends to reduce the effect of the tragedy (see the question on page 70) you must look at the scenes of Polonius at home, where the humour of the incessant pompous speeches merges with the coldness of the domestic tyrant and the compulsive spy. It is not a nice, foolish, funny old man who is speaking to Ophelia at the end of this scene.

Coursework

It is amusing to note that Laertes and Polonius, each full of his own wisdom, advise Ophelia to avoid Hamlet for opposite reasons. Compare lines 19–28 with lines 123–126 for their views on the amount of freedom Hamlet has as a prince.

Family obedience

The reaction and behaviour of Ophelia here are subject to speculation. Is she characterless, obeying her father without thinking, or does she have opinions of her own which she dare not express? Certainly Laertes' behaviour towards his father shows a tradition of obedience that Ophelia can be expected to share: family disputes do not scar the Polonius family as they do the Royal House of Denmark. Shakespeare deliberately gives Ophelia very few lines of ordinary dialogue, and even by the end of the play she is almost more a symbolic figure than a material one.

The family

Ophelia's brief questions to Laertes are neutral in tone, but her obedience to his instructions (lines 45–46) is followed by her warning to him to follow his own advice. Is the tone earnest, argumentative or gently mocking? Look at the inflated diction ('puff'd and reckless libertine' and 'primrose path of dalliance') and use of alliteration ('primrose path' and 'recks not his own rede').

With her father Ophelia seems unwilling to repeat what Laertes has said to her, but obedience prevails. Look at all the brief replies she gives to questions about Hamlet, and note the words she uses about him: 'affection', 'honourable', 'holy'. There is no indication that Ophelia thinks that her father is right, but every indication that she thinks it right to obey him: she says that she does not know what she should think and, after 20 lines of silence, concludes, 'I shall obey, my lord.'

Act 1, Scenes 4 and 5

The Ghost appears to Hamlet and demands revenge.

The drama of the supernatural

There is a temptation to discuss Shakespeare's plays purely in terms of the study: imagery, themes, structure, etc. It is important to remember that their effectiveness on stage is just as important. The dramatic presentation of the Ghost is chillingly effective, focusing the audience's attention (as well as Hamlet's) on the message that will shape the whole play.

The atmosphere is established before the Ghost's entry: the cold midnight, trumpets sounding, big guns firing (though not in war). The Ghost surprises us while Hamlet is discoursing on faults in Man, and is first of all a mere presence as Hamlet's shock and fear draw in the audience: 'Angels and ministers of grace defend us!' Tension builds: will the Ghost speak?

Revenge

With Hamlet alone it does speak, beginning with words that emphasise the significance of the message ('Mark me') and the shortness of time before it returns to torment ('My hour is almost come…'). Only after this preamble does the Ghost embark on its tale of horror, announcing itself ('I am thy father's spirit') and beginning with the sufferings of Purgatory – remember these when Hamlet refuses to kill his uncle at prayer and (he thinks) send him to Heaven.

Though we never truly doubt that the Ghost is speaking the truth, it is only in Scene 5, line 9, that it identifies itself, and part of the dramatic effect depends upon the fear the mortals have of what it intends to do.

Hamlet

Hamlet finds it in 'questionable shape' (that is, a shape that invites questions), but still believes it may be a 'goblin' (demon). Horatio fears it may lead Hamlet to danger and possess his soul, and the re-entry of Horatio and Marcellus in Scene 5 is full of concern for Hamlet's welfare. Think about how this contributes both to the drama of these scenes and to our assessment of Hamlet's character.

Diction and imagery

The news the Ghost brings is remarkable enough, though not entirely surprising to Hamlet. 'O, my prophetic soul! My uncle!', he says, which at least means that he has predicted that his uncle is evil. However, the Ghost's dramatic news is intensified by the diction and imagery with which it is expressed. Even before he starts his story, two speeches in particular have created an atmosphere of heightened intensity. Look at Hamlet's speech from Scene 4, line 39 onwards and note how the weighty diction conveys a sense of awe in death and funeral: 'sepulchre', 'inurn'd', 'ponderous', and you can find other examples. In the Ghost's first long speech (Scene 5, line 9 onwards) note how Shakespeare conveys the horrors of Purgatory by creating images of human reaction, culminating in the simile, 'Like quills upon the fretful

Revenge

porpentine'. This speech ends with the headline announcement of the conclusion of his story: murder!

The mood is set by such words as 'foul', 'strange' and 'unnatural' and the image of the 'fat weed… on Lethe wharf' (Lethe being the river of forgetfulness in the Classical Underworld).

Corruption

Thereafter the dominant images are of corruption (and, to an extent, its opposite, virtue), from the serpent and the incestuous beast to the 'luxury and damned incest' of line 83. Make a list of all the examples you can find and divide them into categories of corruption: sexual corruption, bodily decay, the corruption of sin, poison.

The mood of these scenes is by no means all solemn. The hysteria of the later stages, hinting at madness and painfully funny, creates a mood almost unique to *Hamlet*. The old question ('Is Hamlet mad?') can be raised here. As the Ghost leaves and Hamlet vows to remember him before all other things, he refers to his head (and, by implication, the world) as 'distracted': mad.

Certainly the soliloquy before the re-entry of his companions seems

Madness

unbalanced: note the reference to 'most pernicious woman', which suggests that incest still plagues him as much as murder. His 'wild and whirling' conversation with Horatio, with its unfulfilled hints at revelation and its sudden farewells, leads up to the most bizarre episode: the swearing of the oaths encouraged by the Ghost from beneath the stage. Hamlet suddenly treats the Ghost with jocular familiarity: 'truepenny', 'old mole', 'worthy pioner'.

Coursework

Tragedy

A moment of great solemnity is broken into by what can be seen as undergraduate clowning. Somehow, though, Hamlet's intensity is conveyed through this wildly unconventional scene.

Confusingly, and typically, Hamlet now warns Horatio that he will 'put an antic disposition on': the unbalanced prince will pretend to be mad and scholars will debate what is real madness and what assumed.

What is certain is the expectation of the audience at the end of Act 1. The

Revenge

assumed madness is likely to be a stage to the pursuit of revenge. We (and Hamlet) really have no doubt that the Ghost is telling truth and that, within the society presented here, his duty is revenge. The memorable couplet, 'The time is out of joint. O cursed spite/That ever I was born to set it right', makes clear that Hamlet's role is that of avenger and that he is ill-fitted to that role.

■ Self-test questions Act 1

Who? Why? What? How? Where? When?
1 Who are described as 'liegemen to the Dane' and by whom?
2 Whose beard was 'a sable silver'd'?
3 Who seeks the King's permission to return to France?
4 Why must the Ghost depart in both 1.1 and 1.5?
5 What custom is 'more honour'd in the breach than the observance'?
6 What instructions does Polonius give Ophelia about Hamlet?
7 How does Marcellus propose to stop the Ghost in 1.1?
8 Where does Hamlet wish to return to?
9 Where is Laertes going when he pauses to advise Ophelia?
10 When, according to Horatio, did the graves stand 'tenantless'?

Complete the quotes
Find the following important quotations in Act 1, identify the speaker and complete the phrase or sentence.
1 'How weary, stale, flat and unprofitable ...'
2 'With mirth in funeral ...'
3 'A little more than kin ...'
4 'This above all ...'
5 'The time is out of joint. O cursed spite ...'
6 'O villain, villain ...'
7 'Murder most foul ...'
8 'He may not, as unvalu'd persons do ...'
9 'like a puff'd and reckless libertine ...'
10 'To post/With such dexterity ...'

Prove it!
1 Find evidence that Hamlet suspects the King of evil (not necessarily of the murder) before the Ghost's evidence.
2 Prove that the country is in a state of readiness for war with Norway.
3 What evidence is there of Laertes' behaviour following his father's example?
4 Prove that Claudius wishes at this stage to gain Hamlet's co-operation, not his destruction.

Signs and themes
Find examples in this act of images of drunkenness, corruption and deception, and comment on how they are presented and what we can learn from them.

Act 2, Scene 1

Polonius sends Reynaldo to Paris and receives news from Ophelia.

Why include Reynaldo?

The opening section with Reynaldo can be a victim of cutting in stage productions. It is worth considering why Shakespeare included it: there is no suggestion that Polonius is acting on information received, or that Reynaldo found any evidence of Laertes' wildness. The most enjoyable feature of the scene is the comedy at Polonius's expense, particularly when his sentences become so confused that even he does not know where he has reached. Is this really necessary, though? Does it perhaps unbalance our view of Polonius, who must not be seen just as an amiable bumbler?

In a more serious light, though amusingly presented, it does reveal important aspects of Polonius's character. He is a man committed to spying: his motto might be 'By indirections find directions out'. He is reluctant to trust his spying to anyone else: clearly he cannot go to Paris, but his detailed instructions even include the exact words that Reynaldo should use. These qualities will ultimately lead to Polonius's death. Also, this

The court

scene provides an insight into his personal morality. 'Drabbing' (visiting whores) he finds just acceptable, so long as it is not unrestrained. A sort of respectability must be maintained; morality itself is less important.

Another reason for this scene is to allow the audience to consider the passage of time. If Polonius is sending money and letters to Laertes, some time must have passed since the events of Act 1 which occupy little more than 24 hours. To move from Hamlet seeing the Ghost to Ophelia bringing news of Hamlet, apparently mad, would have been confusing.

Corruption

Hamlet visits Ophelia

Like Ophelia's death, this is a famous scene, much loved by artists, which exists purely in narrative. The scene is the natural consequence of two decisions in

Act 1. Firstly, Polonius told his obedient daughter to have nothing to do with Hamlet. The fact that she 'denied his access' has provided further confirmation of the fickleness of women and has prompted this action. He has chosen to appear 'with his doublet all unbrac'd' and 'with a look so piteous' as

Madness

part of his 'antic disposition'. Remember that it is Ophelia (at her father's prompting) who has rejected Hamlet; the image of Ophelia as the pure woman rejected in love is at some variance with the facts.

However, there are deeper questions about Hamlet's motives. Is he so madly in love that he is deeply affected by rejection? Why, then, has he not mentioned Ophelia up to this point, even in soliloquy? Is Ophelia merely the excuse?

Ophelia enters 'so affrighted' and there is no reason to suppose her not to be afraid. However, compared to the sense of disturbance in the speech of other characters, notably Hamlet, her speech seems very orderly. The diction invites a sense of pathos: a typical adjective is 'piteous' and there is a detailed description of a conventional image of a love-sick youth, with stockings round his ankles, sighing and thrusting his hand across his brow. However, though many of the words suggest intense emotion, the verse is remarkably orderly.

In the verse passages, Shakespeare habitually uses blank verse: that is, unrhymed verse written in iambic pentameter. Iambic pentameter is a line of verse of ten syllables, with five stresses falling on the even syllables. Shakespeare's use of it is generally very flexible, and intense emotion causes the verse patterns to break up. In this scene Ophelia speaks for the most part in regular iambic pentameter, with many lines being 'end-stopped'; that is to say, the natural breaks in the sense, often indicated by punctuation marks, occur at the end of lines. This gives the impression of orderly speech.

Examine the speech beginning on line 87: 'He *took* me *by* the *wrist* and *held* me *hard*.' This line is a perfect iambic pentameter ended with a full stop. Continue through the rest of the speech and see how it continues: of course, all breaks in the sense are not marked by a full stop. Then compare it with a speech of Hamlet: 1.2. 129–159, 1.4. 13–38 and 1.5. 173–188 are three examples you could choose.

Act 2, Scene 2

This is the major court scene of the play: from the arrival of Rosencrantz and Guildenstern to the arrival of the Players, via scenes with ambassadors, Polonius and others.

From this point to Hamlet's departure for England there is a free-wheeling continuity to the play, though one can imagine gaps in the action at certain points: the performance of the play is to be the night after the arrival of the Players, for instance. However, this scene is continuous, while still being divisible into separate sections, often of different character. The interesting structural point is that the King and Queen never share the stage with Hamlet. Between Hamlet's promise to remain at Elsinore and the play scene they circle each other without their paths actually crossing. Here, as Hamlet enters at line 167, the Queen notes his arrival and she and Claudius depart, doubtless in the opposite direction, at line 170. The continuity of the scene is provided by the King for the first 170 lines, then, with Polonius bridging the gap to Hamlet, by the Prince for the rest of the scene.

The King: the public face and private indecision

The opening 170 lines see the King in three situations: welcoming Rosencrantz and Guildenstern, greeting the ambassadors from Norway on their successful return and discussing Hamlet's madness with the Queen and Polonius. The first two situations reveal him as comfortable in his public role; the third betrays private anxieties and indecision.

The court

Note the care that characterises speech patterns in the first section of the scene: speakers constantly flatter each other with 'good', 'gentle', 'gracious' and more extended compliments. Is the reference to 'your (i.e. Gertrude's) son' (not 'our') a slip from this image of bland goodness? Probably not – no one else is there to hear it.

Coursework

The first 39 lines are an exercise in political blandness delivered by the playwright with more than a hint of irony. The King speaks formally, projecting the character of a concerned uncle/father who simply wishes to know the truth ('open'd') and put things right ('within our remedy'). The Queen emphasises their regard for Rosencrantz and Guildenstern and both Majesties use such humble words and phrases as 'entreat' and 'if it will please you'. The young men, however, know their place and use words like 'command' and 'obey'. Though Guildenstern is careless enough to use the word 'practices' (deceits, tricks), the court in this scene is a picture of concerned and considerate parenthood and monarchy.

Examiner's tip

Your essay on revenge (question 1, page 73) will take account of Fortinbras's pursuit of revenge. Though he continues in martial vein, it does, in fact, end early and tamely. Perhaps the most interesting comparison here is Fortinbras's obedience to his uncle: 'Receives rebuke from Norway and... Makes vow before his uncle...'

Examination

The brief ambassadors scene, often cut, is, however, of some importance for the plot. With the removal of the threat posed by Fortinbras, the distractions of war are avoided, but Fortinbras himself is still there, and he will cross Denmark and provide another parallel to Hamlet and become the future King of Denmark. Does the scene also imply Claudius's skill as a diplomat? Are we to see Claudius as a capable king who has gained power the wrong way, or is he evil, corrupt and a disgrace to his country?

Interestingly, although Polonius is the soul of respect ('my good liege', 'my dear Majesty', etc.), he sets the agenda in all the conversations about Hamlet. Even in the gap between the departure of Rosencrantz and Guildenstern and the entry of the ambassadors, he announces that he has found 'the very cause of Hamlet's lunacy' – the King wishes to hear it, but Polonius insists that he must wait until he has seen the ambassadors.

In the main discussion of Hamlet's case (lines 86–167) both Claudius and Gertrude offer little more than questions, though Gertrude is briefly annoyed with Polonius's prolixity and Claudius twice supplies approving answers to his self-regarding questions. When the King says decisively, 'We will try it', he is accepting Polonius's scheme to extend spying by observing Hamlet and Ophelia.

Madness

Comedy of expression

One result of Polonius dominating the scene is that, quite unexpectedly, verbal comedy resurfaces. Polonius seems unable to speak without indulging in wordplay and definitions. The most absurd example is the piece of nonsense beginning 'That he is mad, 'tis true'; the neatest piece of irony is his claim that 'brevity is the soul of wit'. Examine for yourself the self-satisfied wordplay about time, madness and effect/defect.

Polonius now turns literary critic, delaying his news still further by commenting on the style of Hamlet's letter. What of the letter itself? You might think that, for a young man of the intellect and imagination of Hamlet, it is rather disappointing. He is, indeed, 'ill at these numbers' (poor at writing verse). His use of the affected contemporary phrase about the 'machine' (his body) rather conflicts with his general strictures about plainness of speech. Is Hamlet again playing a role, or is this the way he usually expresses himself in love? There is no definite answer: the matter simply throws up the further question of whether the letter was written before Polonius's prohibition or was recently written for him to intercept and misinterpret.

Hamlet

Polonius's confidence is in proportion to his error. His account of the love, rejection and decline of Hamlet is full of convincing detail and presents him as a positive dominating figure. 'Take this from this' (head from shoulders), he asserts, if he is wrong. See how many other examples you can find of his belief in his own infallibility. The irony which the audience can appreciate is that he is totally misled and the Queen (not regarded as particularly clever or subtle) has already perceived the truth of it. In lines 56 and 57 she blames his madness on 'his father's death and our o'er-hasty

The court

marriage', very accurate as far as it goes: she cannot be expected to know of the Ghost or see through the 'antic disposition'.

The family

Much as we enjoy the folly of Polonius, this is a good time for another warning against seeing him purely as a comic character. The next stage in the spying will be the occasion for him to 'loose my daughter to him', a chillingly impersonal turn of phrase.

Spies, deceptions and delays

One of the consistently debatable issues of *Hamlet* is the extent to which the Prince is too indecisive in carrying out the Ghost's orders and the reasons why

Revenge

he delays so much. Traditionally, commentators used the 'No delay, no play' motif, which justifies it purely in terms of stagecraft, not in terms of the imagined character of Hamlet. Some critics claim that he has had no opportunity to act: hardly likely in view of the amount of time that has passed between Acts 1 and 2 and the ease with which Laertes and Hamlet himself gain

potentially lethal access to the King later in the play. In simple terms we know of Hamlet's indecision and delay because he admits it himself, but it is exaggerated because of Shakespeare's inclusive approach to material in this play.

Coursework

Tragedy

In the question on page 70 you are asked to consider if irrelevant material reduces the impact of tragedy. For two-thirds of Act 2, Scene 2, tense exchanges alternate with absurd comedy, discussion of the theatre and extended recitations, culminating in a highly charged soliloquy. Does the impression given of Hamlet's inertia increase or reduce tension?

In Acts 2 and 3 Hamlet is active, but the action is slowed by the inclusion of a series of extended dialogue scenes whose length is justified less by their relevance to the plot than by their high entertainment value and depiction of the character of Hamlet. So it is in the last 400 lines of Act 2.

Hamlet's ability to see through the claims and impostures of the King's

Hamlet

representatives is acute. In turn and in different ways Polonius and Rosencrantz and Guildenstern are humiliated though, for now at least, Hamlet keeps on polite enough terms with his old school friends to chat about theatre with them. More important to the plot is the fact that he plants enough ideas in the heads of all three to spread confusion among his enemies.

The fascination for the student is in attempting to discern if there are any elements of truth in these deceptions: there is no 'correct' answer, but long and detailed discussions can be had on whether he is really as world-weary as 'What piece of work is a man' suggests.

Hamlet's first dialogue with Polonius in this scene (lines 171–219) begins with a surprise to audience and Polonius alike: 'You are a fishmonger.' Contemporary myth about fishmongers' daughters suggested that they were especially likely to breed (hence later references to 'good kissing carrion' and conception), but the humour also depends on the absurdity of the rejoinder. Even better is the fact that Polonius (who, you remember, has never been wrong!) takes it literally. Hamlet's 'Into my grave?' as a response to a request to walk out of the air is calculated to send Polonius scurrying into mistaken interpretations. Examine the whole of this section and see how many examples you can find of Hamlet taking the opportunity to insult and deceive the old man.

The family

Examination

Examiner's tip

Any examination of the characters who betray Hamlet (question 2, page 75) should take note of those whose betrayal is itself betrayed by his perception and their clumsiness, notably Rosencrantz and Guildenstern. From this first scene with Hamlet to their voyage to England, their attempts to betray their old friend are transparent and ineffective.

The opening of the scene with Rosencrantz and Guildenstern (lines 222 onwards) is subtler because Hamlet does not yet know the reason for their arrival and needs to find out if they were 'sent for'. We begin with jolly exchanges, as between old friends who are not quite *good* friends, with the conversation witty, sparkling and a little strained: the mildly rude joke about  being Fortune's 'privates', for instance. Nonchalantly and at irregular intervals, Hamlet poses tests for them: Denmark a prison; bad dreams; a conversation about ambition. Their replies are bland and artificial: they are saying what they should, what the King would wish. Casually, Hamlet asks, as a friend, what they are doing there, then springs the trap: 'Were you not sent for?' Soon they are speechless and Hamlet can present his own version of his mental state for delivery to Claudius: 'I have of late... lost all my mirth... Man delights not me', and later the mysterious and deliberately confusing 'I am but mad north-north-west'.

The court

Madness

The players

The elements in this scene that could, most evidently, be seen as redundant are those concerning the Players: the dialogue with Rosencrantz and Guildenstern and then with Polonius, and the mighty speeches about Pyrrhus. The performance of the play will, of course, be highly significant, but the time devoted to discussing the theatre may be seen as excessive. Yet, in *Hamlet*, some of the less strictly relevant scenes are among the most memorable and also provide some of the most fascinating insights into the Elizabethan world Shakespeare inhabited.

The first mention of the Players (line 314) arises naturally in conversation, and from there to their actual entry over 100 lines later the main topic of conversation is contemporary theatre, with Shakespeare's comments often satirical.

Hamlet's complexity of character is well shown here. It is difficult to

 imagine any other tragic hero in pursuit of revenge who could pause to chat with easy familiarity and keen knowledge to a group of actors about their careers and their art. Examine his dialogue with the Players and find all the examples you can of conversation where Hamlet treats them as equals: he even knows enough about the ways of actors to warn them off

Hamlet

mocking Polonius (a line doubtless delivered with a conspiratorial wink).

It is Hamlet who begins the performance of speeches from the Play of Troy. What are we to think of these speeches? The blank verse seems horribly over-written compared with Shakespeare's own, and we do not have to take Hamlet's praise as Shakespeare's. Is it a parody of Kyd and other tragic writers, especially Marlowe and Nashe's *Tragedy of Dido* on a similar subject? Even Hamlet finds 'mobbled' a bit much; Polonius, of course, is impressed by the word. The diction constantly makes melodramatic demands on our emotions ('dread', 'dismal', 'horribly') and strains at heightened images ('eyes like carbuncles'). See what further examples you can find.

It is of great significance that this verse can, however, strike at the emotions, not least those of the actor who is moved to tears. Shakespeare is clear about the power of theatre: actors are 'the abstract and brief chroniclers of the time.'

There is no doubt that these scenes about the theatre are included for their own sake, but there is much that can be applied to the main plot. The theme of appearance and reality is never far away in *Hamlet* and theatrical illusion makes another contribution to this. The presence of the actors leads to various important comments from Hamlet. His first words on hearing of the Players are, 'He that plays the king shall be welcome', an ominous anticipation of the insertion of some twelve or sixteen lines as planned at the end of the scene. The popularity of the child actors is another example of the world turned upside down – no odder than Claudius being King of Denmark.

Revenge

The speeches of Priam and Pyrrhus present an exaggerated commentary on the events of the play: the death of a King, a grieving Queen. This is especially true of Pyrrhus, who joins a group of four avengers in *Hamlet*. Apart from leading up to the play scene, the other main purpose of this scene is its effect on Hamlet.

'O what a rogue and peasant slave am I!'

Let us consider why Hamlet's soliloquies are so effective. Perhaps their greatest strength is that they chart the developing and changing thoughts of a character capable of deep introspection. A speech like Edmund's 'Thou, nature, art my goddess' in *King Lear* announces him in bravura style, but Hamlet becomes a different person (or, at least, changes his perspective) in the course of a soliloquy and even surprises himself with his thought processes. Furthermore, the means of expression changes along with the subject of thought.

Hamlet

At first (to line 551) Hamlet describes the Player's acting with plenty of words that appeal to the emotions ('monstrous', 'passion', 'tears', etc.), but generally in a controlled form – mostly end-stopped lines, some of them nicely balanced, such as 'Tears in his eyes, distraction in his aspect'. This relatively orderly pattern begins to break up with the exclamation 'And all for nothing!', and the first of the very short lines in this speech: 'For Hecuba!' At this point Hamlet is turning his thoughts back to himself and, when he resumes consideration of the Player, order is restored in the verse, though the diction is full of disordered words like 'mad', 'amaze' and 'appal'. The line 'Yet I' disturbs the regular rhythm again: Hamlet's mind is at its most distracted when he thinks of himself and what he has failed to do. You will notice that, despite his admiration for the Player, this comparison is, as yet, leading nowhere: what good would it do Hamlet to 'drown the stage with tears ... and amaze indeed the faculties of eyes and ears'?

From lines 561 to 578 a speech that began as a fairly well-organised comparison between theatrical and real passion completely loses shape as Hamlet does not know where his self-disgust is leading him: a series of self-insults, a recollection of his dead father, a questioning of his courage, a descent into agonised curses of Claudius and, finally, 'Why, what an ass am I!', which is both the culmination of his self-abasement and a 'pull-yourself-together' rallying cry.

Corruption

Through all these tortured mental wanderings the expression is equally tortured: broken sentences, verse that dissolves into the single syllable line 'Ha!', questions, exclamations, ever more colloquial expression and contractions ('I should ha' fatted', for instance).

In lines 578 to 584 he bullies his brain back into action, now cursing his previous descent into cursing, until finally, with a 'Hum' that means 'Let's think', he launches into the precise planning of lines 584–601. Diction and sentence construction are brisk, the verse ordered, though thrusting forward too much to be end-stopped. Now the play scene is conceived. The question remains whether this is action on Hamlet's part. You need to balance two convincing viewpoints, both put forward by critics. In the first place, the statement that the Ghost 'may be a devil' (line 595) fits in well with what Hamlet has actually witnessed and it may be seen as action to set about proving its veracity. On the other hand, setting up a play may be seen as a typical substitute for real action: the excitement of doing something distracts from Hamlet's anxiety about the deed itself. In support of this is the fact that, dramatically, the Ghost always seems honest, but at least the play scene prompts decisive action, though not quite in the way Hamlet hopes.

■ Self-test questions Act 2

Who? Why? What? How? Where? When?
1   Who is sent to spy on Laertes in Paris?
2   Who are Priam, Hecuba and Pyrrhus?
3   Who states that the world is a prison?
4   Why have Rosencrantz and Guildenstern been sent for?
5   Why have the actors left the city?
6   What is the Hyrcanian beast?
7   What does Polonius call 'a vile phrase'?
8   How, according to Hamlet, should Polonius treat the actors?
9   Where was Ophelia when Hamlet came to her?
10 When was it ever proved that Polonius made a mistake of judgement, according to the King and Polonius himself?

Complete the quotes
Find the following important quotations in Act 2, identify the speaker and complete the phrase or sentence.
1   'That he is mad 'tis true ...'
2   'And then, sir, does a this – a does ...'
3   'As if he had been loosed ...'
4   'What piece of work is a man ...'
5   'What's Hecuba to him ...'
6   'Happy in that ...'
7   'Conception is a blessing ...'
8   'Your bait of falsehood ...'
9   'Though this be madness ...
10 'let them be well used, for ...'

The theme of madness
1   What are the first signs of Hamlet adopting his 'antic disposition'?
2   What interpretation does Polonius give of the causes of Hamlet's madness?

3　In speaking to the King, what stages does Polonius imagine for this madness?
4　What is Polonius's interpretation of Hamlet's behaviour to him in 2.2, lines 171 onwards?
5　What account of his state of mind does Hamlet give Rosencrantz and Guildenstern to pass to the King? What definition does he give simply to warn and confuse them?
6　Give two examples that Hamlet cites of a world gone mad.
7　Whom does Hamlet describe as having 'distraction (madness) in his aspect'?

The theatre
Identify or explain the following:
1　A famous Roman actor.
2　Two Latin playwrights, the first famed for tragedy, the second for comedy and farce.
3　References to the Children of the Chapel, an acting company in London in 1600.
4　The probable original of 'Hercules and his load'.
5　A reference to boy actors playing women's parts.

Act 3, Scene 1

The so-called nunnery scene.

Plot and counter-plot

The court is now a centre of intrigue. Who is on the offensive? No sooner has Hamlet planned to 'catch the conscience of the King' by means of the play than the King and Polonius set their trap to find out the cause of Hamlet's madness. Both the King and Hamlet feel they need 'grounds more relative' before they can take action. When Hamlet finally acts, though not in the way he intends, the King is freed to react instantly. Ironically, in the opening dialogue with Rosencrantz and Guildenstern and Polonius, the King agrees to the play as part of the attempt to reform Hamlet, when it is the main plank of Hamlet's intrigue against him.

The court
The court here is full of espionage and intrigue. The King and Queen interrogate Rosencrantz and Guildenstern, then the King turns to the more secret operation: 'Sweet Gertrude, leave us too', where Hamlet will be confronted by Ophelia, 'as 'twere by accident'. But the Prince, of course, has his own plans.

Coursework

The main body of the scene is Hamlet's most famous soliloquy, followed by the intensity of the meeting with Ophelia. The opening 55 lines are low key, a necessary emotional respite between the two soliloquies, but full of telling details.

Madness

The King, for instance, sees Hamlet's madness as 'turbulent and dangerous': having gained power by violence, all he wants is an end to violence, but it is difficult to halt the process, once begun. Note also that he suspects that Hamlet's madness may be assumed: 'puts on' is later supported by Guildenstern's 'crafty madness'.

This scene gives the first hints that the King suffers with his conscience. When Polonius, for no particular reason except his love of moralising, comments on the human tendency to hypocrisy, Claudius is moved to a brief

Corruption

self-torturing aside. The telling metaphor, 'My most painted word', a comparison to the painted face of a whore, is an image that recalls Hamlet's disgust at the world. Note also that Claudius's treatment of Gertrude suggests a need to spare her a guilty involvement: he asks her to leave and assures her that he and Polonius are 'lawful espials'. The Queen and Ophelia genuinely hope that Hamlet will come to his senses. Only Polonius, stage managing the whole thing and treating his daughter like a prop for the scene, lacks a human dimension here.

'To be or not to be': Hamlet and suicide

The most famous soliloquy in Shakespeare's plays is technically not a soliloquy, a speech delivered by one character on his/her own, for Ophelia is also on stage. However, since he sees Ophelia for the first time in line 88, it is clearly a speech expressing honestly Hamlet's thought processes and should be regarded as a soliloquy. There is, of course, a convention that soliloquies convey thoughts, rather than spoken words, like an extended aside, so we are not to imagine that Ophelia, Claudius or Polonius realise that Hamlet is philosophising about suicide.

This might be a suitable point to think about the staging of the

The court

eavesdropping. Every director has a decision to make about whether Hamlet is aware of Polonius and Claudius during the dialogue with Ophelia. Are his words served up for the King's consumption or are they simply part of the 'antic disposition'? Does he openly expose the listeners, or suggest awareness by reaction, or play the scene regardless? Conventional wisdom would incline towards some sort of discovery at line 130: 'Where's your father?', but it is a matter of interpretation.

Hamlet

In the soliloquy, however, Hamlet is speaking his thoughts, aware of no one else. The tone is calmer, more reflective, than in either of the previous soliloquies and there is a sense of thinking through a problem without being distracted into exclamations of fury or disgust. Much more generalised, it lacks the personal references, both to 'I' and, in various cankered epithets, to Claudius. The question for you to decide, therefore, is whether Hamlet is seriously considering suicide. Previously he has dismissed the possibility because 'the Everlasting' has banned 'self-slaughter', but on the other hand the opening line seems to pose the simple question: 'Shall I commit suicide?'. Both Dover Wilson and A C Bradley consider Hamlet to be thinking of suicide, but other interpretations range from comparing the value of killing himself and Claudius (Wilson Knight) to debating whether to stage the play (Alex Newell). The theme, however, is certainly the value of human life – is it worth living? – and the expression is more philosophical than passionate. Each director/actor/teacher/student will decide how seriously Hamlet is considering ending his own life, but it would be foolish to ignore the calm, if melancholy, tone and the evidence of the Act 1, Scene 2, soliloquy.

Hamlet

Hamlet's depressed view of life can be judged from the fact that none of the reasons for preserving it concern the value or enjoyment of life. The appeal of the speech depends partly on its mixture of simplicity of diction and precision of images. All Hamlet's soliloquies have striking openings: none, though, compares with this stark string of monosyllables. Key points are marked by memorably plain phrases: the repeated 'to die, to sleep' (first time welcoming, second time leading to a frightening possibility) or 'ay, there's the rub'. On the other hand, strikingly concrete images tell of both life's sufferings and the terrors of the grave. The list of life's injustices (lines 70–74) or the idea of the afterlife as the dreams of death (line 65) are good examples; see what others you can find. The argument is clear-cut and the conclusion logical. Why should we suffer life when we could find peace? Because it might not be peace. Therefore we 'bear those ills we have'.

Revenge

Though the speech remains impersonal and philosophical, it is very tempting to relate lines 83–88 to Hamlet's present situation. 'The pale cast of thought', we imagine him thinking, is preventing 'enterprises of great pitch and moment': not suicide, but revenge. This interpretation is perfectly acceptable, so long as you remember that the 'conscience' that turns us into cowards is not so much conscience as we understand it as the process of thought: consciousness.

Hamlet and Ophelia

One of the stranger elements of the Hamlet–Ophelia relationship is the small amount of time they spend together on stage and the nature of their conversations. Typically, their talk is in prose, dominated by Hamlet's loss of faith in women, whether expressed in disgust at sex or (in the next scene) coarse propositioning. The audience is thus forced to construct an imaginary idealised romance between the two which is reflected in many of Ophelia's speeches in the absence of Hamlet, as in this scene, where lines 153–163 are a touching testament to Hamlet's qualities of mind and body and Ophelia's grief at seeing

41

this 'most sovereign reason' 'blasted with ecstasy' (beside himself). On the basis of speeches like this, one is tempted to find Hamlet's treatment of Ophelia cruel, but remember that she knows (and he probably suspects) who the unseen listeners are.

This scene begins in slightly formal blank verse: Ophelia speaks very correctly, using 'my lord' constantly, and Hamlet initially responds with gentle distraction. Note, by the way, that this is their first meeting for 'this many a day'. Why should her attempt (which she makes instantly, with little pretence at ordinary conversation) to return his keepsakes prompt such a violent response? Perhaps Hamlet recognises the originator of the scheme: does the style of the neat little couplet seem familiar? 'Take these again; for to the noble mind/Rich gifts wax poor when givers prove unkind.' Immediately, though Ophelia remains the model of politeness, Hamlet abandons verse for prose

Madness

and a certain savagery of expression. His speech is disjointed and the use of 'nunnery' in the dual sense of 'convent' and slang for 'brothel' can be disconcerting, as can the several false exits, where he bids Ophelia farewell, then returns to the insults, but the King is right: this does not resemble madness. The themes are consistent, if disturbed. Women, particularly beautiful women, have no honour ('honesty'); all mankind of both sexes is full of secret sins; rumour, scandal and female deception disgust him.

Corruption

The man who believes 'Frailty, thy name is woman!' and who debates internally the merit of suicide is here expressing his own views, though the method of expression may be assumed. Some lines seem aimed at the hidden listeners: how do you interpret the lines about banning marriage (lines 148–151) and the line, 'Those that are married already – all but one – shall live'?

Towards the confrontation

It is common in Shakespeare's tragedies to reach a first climax in Act 3 before tension eases back in Act 4, often with a number of scenes in different locations, followed by the major climax of Act 5. Such is certainly the case in *Hamlet*, with Act 3 virtually continuous and climaxing with the play scene, the King at Prayer and the murder of Polonius. Note, now, that each scene ends with references to the next stage of the plot. Act 2, Scene 2, looked forward to the play scene; now a similar effect occurs in Act 3, Scene 1. The final section has a self-obsessed ruthlessness. The King has heard enough. Hamlet is to go to England, though as yet we do not know the full story: he is simply going to collect the Danegeld.

Polonius is still convinced that he is right and, virtually ignoring his daughter, plans to eavesdrop on a meeting between Hamlet and Gertrude. These three plots placed together – play, eavesdropping in the Queen's chamber and sending Hamlet to England – produce violent confrontations and the first wave of killings in the play.

Act 3, Scene 2

The play scene.

Hamlet, Horatio and the Players

Hamlet

While in the presence of the court, during, before and after the play, Hamlet is restless, distracted, frequently offensive, with even the Queen being the victim of one barbed comment. It is pleasing to find him in two contrasting situations before the entry of the court (line 92), behaving pleasantly and normally in two totally different conversational veins. The first 45 lines are a rasping critique of styles of theatre, delivered with an overbearing confidence, maybe, but very entertaining nonetheless.

Then all is serious and Hamlet is sane and controlled, delivering a serious message to Horatio in assured blank verse. We have not seen Horatio since Act 1 and now Hamlet clearly lays down what his role is to be. Why does Hamlet need a 'man who is not passion's slave'? What does Horatio, previously seen as the sceptic philosopher, now have to contribute to the play?

The court

From the entry of the court the intensity builds to an unbearable pitch: none of the main characters involved in watching *The Murder of Gonzago* (or *The Mousetrap*) is unchanged by the experience. This great set piece is literally central to the play and can be compared with the events next time the court gathers for entertainment: the duel between Hamlet and Laertes. In both cases the amusement will be ultimately fatal (this time on a less drastic scale, for the moment). In both cases secret plots are being hatched beneath the courtly surface: Hamlet writes a speech; Claudius poisons a sword tip and a drink.

Hamlet at court

Madness

Hamlet's behaviour is not mad, but it is not normal. What is obvious from the outset is his burning contempt for Claudius, Polonius and Rosencrantz and Guildenstern. Does he feel contempt also for Ophelia? Certainly his conversation with her reeks of disgust: at her, or himself, or women, or sexual desire?

He expresses the contempt and disgust freely because it matches his assumed madness and also provokes reactions, his aim at this point – what has he to lose, anyway? You can chart this right through the scene. On the King's entry, Hamlet can barely trouble himself to speak to him: a bitter comment about his inferior position at court, and he has finished talking to Claudius until the increasingly excited comments mid-play, when he pretends

Corruption

to reassure the King about the content. Polonius is set up for a laboured pun on 'Brutus'/'brute' and 'Capitol'/'capital', perhaps a glancing blow at Polonius's own wearisome wordplay. Later, with Polonius, Hamlet cannot even bother to pretend to make sense: Polonius is under orders to flatter the dangerous madman, so Hamlet insults his intelligence with the nonsensical series of cloud shapes. As for Rosencrantz and Guildenstern, they are to find his ferocious frankness on the matter of pipes rather too much for them.

Examination

Examiner's tip
Question 2, page 75, asks you to consider the way in which Hamlet's betrayers betray themselves. With Rosencrantz and Guildenstern it is particularly abrupt and painful. They betray their mission by word, gesture and expression. 'You would play upon me,' says Hamlet; their secret is betrayed and soon it will lead to their deaths.

Hamlet's conversations with Ophelia, and his comments to her and the others during the play, express his genuinely held feelings (sexual disgust, excitement at trapping the King) while also transmitting coded messages.

The family

Hamlet's rejection of his mother for Ophelia is meant to warn Gertrude that his love cannot be relied on until she clears herself of her connection with guilt, but also it aims to confuse Claudius about the cause of his madness: it worked with Polonius, at least.

After this, barely a speech does not have an obscene meaning, whether obvious or concealed. The intention to 'lie in your lap' leads to 'country matters' (physical love – sex, with an obscene pun), 'nothing' (the male 'thing') between her legs, the need for 'a groaning to take off my edge' and many more.

Corruption

You will normally find language and jokes of this sort only in some of the Shakespearean clowns: here is the hero of the play, a noble prince, expressing himself in this way to a young lady at court. What is the dramatic effect of this, both on the audience and the listeners at court?

Coursework

Tragedy
Here is a particularly potent example of comedy reinforcing the tragic menace of a scene. When Hamlet jests on 'country matters' and announces the dumb-show with alliterative excess as 'miching malicho ... mischief', it is funny, but the unease that spreads through the court reaches the audience.

Occasionally Hamlet deserts the sexual imagery to make allusion to regular themes of his discontent: satirical reference to the air-brushing out of history of his father ('die two months ago and not forgotten yet!') or the frailty of women ('brief ... As woman's love').

The performance

The play is a pastiche of an older, more formal and elaborate dramatic style associated with playwrights like Robert Greene. Shakespeare enjoys himself throughout *Hamlet* in giving impressions, some cruel, of different styles of speech, writing, acting and manners. This is among the less cruel: the rhyming couplets chime on with monotonous regularity, there is no sense of real emotion, but it is written with restraint and dignity until the arrival of Lucianus with his 'Thoughts black, hands apt...'

There are two unsolved problems about the play-within-a-play. Which is Hamlet's 'speech of some dozen or sixteen lines' and, more important, what is the function of the dumb-show? As given in detail after line 133, it anticipates the entire action of the play. It is not uncommon, therefore, for modern productions to shorten it or cut it completely, though it is the only presentation of the end of the story (except in Hamlet's frantic summary as the King rises). To cover the story in mime before a play in this way was not uncommon in Elizabethan times: something not dissimilar happens in the play-within-a-play in *A Midsummer Night's Dream*. The difficulty that remains is explaining why Claudius does not react at first sight of the plot. Perhaps the most sensible answer is that given by Harley Granville-Barker, among others: that Claudius can keep his self-control on seeing his crime once, but a second time is too much for him.

In this scene the focus of drama is on the stage audience: an ingenious theory put forward by Harold Jenkins about the need for a dumb-show suggests that, after one viewing, the theatre audience does not need to watch the actors so much and can concentrate on the stage audience. It is an interesting exercise to go through the text of *The Murder of Gonzago* and surmise how the various characters in the stage audience should react at each point.

The court

This scene offers an insight into the court unravelling. The surface gloss of earlier scenes is beginning to dissolve into helpless unease. Perhaps the greatest achievement of the play scene is to render Polonius speechless. From the smug 'O ho! Do you mark that?' to his call to stop the play, he is silent as his world disintegrates.

Coursework

Reaction

The King departs, 'marvellous distempered', and all the court with him: in the next two scenes we will see in more detail how he, Gertrude and Polonius react to the play. For now Hamlet is alone with Horatio.

Hamlet is now, on his own admission, satisfied that the Ghost told the truth, but is almost too excited at his discovery to act in a connected way. He sends for recorders, recites snatches of ballads (an odd anticipation of the mad Ophelia), pours insults and 'unwholesome answers' on Rosencrantz and Guildenstern, then on Polonius, and is guided towards activity not by his own plans, but by the summons to his mother.

Hamlet

His discourse lurches between the wild and the exact. Note the precisely insulting use of 'trade', and the royal plural in 'Have you any further trade with us?', drawing a line under his friendship with Rosencrantz and Guildenstern. You could also examine in detail the analogy of the recorders (pipes), pursued with much precision and ending with a bitter pun on 'fret' and 'play'.

The final soliloquy is unusual in this play in that there is no changing process of thought, simply the theme of carrying out the Ghost's instructions: to complete revenge, but spare Gertrude suffering. It begins in somewhat melodramatic style, with images more typical of Macbeth. What does the speech show about Hamlet's mind-set at this time?

Revenge

Act 3, Scene 3

The King at prayer.

The opening 35 lines, dealing with sending Hamlet to England and Polonius's spying, make less impact than the two soliloquies later in the scene, but are nonetheless important. They contribute to a sense of the whole castle in bustling confusion, with characters moving hither and yon in pursuit of their own private plots, but they also suggest a decline in Claudius, a breach in the smooth carapace of kingship.

Claudius's decision to implement the journey to England is based on fear, and for once he does not dictate the form of the conversation. Rosencrantz and Guildenstern reassure him at length about his importance and safety; Polonius's news about going to Gertrude's closet is greeted with brief and grateful thanks, in contrast to his rather grudging agreement to the original plan.

The court

The King prays

In a scene divided into three separate sections, the middle one consists of the King's prayer, which proves unsuccessful, as the last couplet of the scene shows. The prayer confirms that he is a villain: near the end he is cursing himself in terms ('O bosom black as death!') not dissimilar to those Hamlet uses about him. Yet this speech is largely responsible for whatever small amount of sympathy we feel for Claudius. Why? Honesty is something we value in a stage character and Claudius, seldom honest, is painfully so here. 'O, my offence is rank, it smells to heaven' is an absolutely uncompromising opening and soon he is making comparisons between himself and Cain, the first murderer.

Claudius also faces unblinkingly the major obstacle to God's forgiveness:

Corruption

how can he ask for forgiveness and still retain the Crown and the Queen, his reasons for committing the murder? It is interesting that, much as he values forgiveness, he does not, of course, consider giving up the Crown. Claudius's dilemma is that of a worldly man who, nevertheless, believes in divine retribution and he gains some measure of sympathy for the impossibility of the situation he has created for himself.

Hamlet fails to kill Claudius

Hamlet

Here is one of the crucial moments of the play, much debated in relation to the character and actions of Hamlet. With hindsight we can say that Hamlet should have killed the King at this point. He does not spare his life ('This physic but prolongs thy sickly days'), and action here would have saved six other lives and placed Hamlet on the throne. Why does he not do it? Shortly he will strike with less reason, but the situation is different: he is striking a hidden enemy, not a man at prayer.

Examiner's tip

Examination

In any study of Hamlet's revenge (question 1, page 73), this is a crucial scene. This is the only time we see Hamlet given an opportunity to kill Claudius (not even planned for – a perfect opportunity). You have to decide how convincing as a reason is Hamlet's refusal to send Claudius to Heaven and his determination to kill him 'drunk asleep or in his rage...'.

There is no 'correct' answer to why Hamlet does not act and you must make up your own mind, first considering the following points. Hamlet appears to have been indecisive for a considerable length of time since Act 1: even though he now has confirmation of guilt, he is still the same person. Nothing would have seemed more offensive to him than to strike a man at prayer. On the other hand, do not dismiss Hamlet's own arguments. When his father's ghost can refer to the 'secrets of my prison-house' that would 'freeze thy young blood' (all because Claudius took him 'grossly, full of bread'), Hamlet is naturally not inclined to send the King to heaven. The scene is full of irony: Claudius's prayers would have been ineffective anyway and his escape helps to bring on Polonius's death. Hamlet draws his sword to kill Claudius and, quite possibly, does not sheathe it again until killing Polonius. In the following scene, after some disturbed but inconclusive lines, the Queen expresses her fear that Hamlet will murder her and calls on Polonius. There is not enough in the lines to justify her reaction, so it must depend on Hamlet's actions or appearance – a still-drawn sword?

Act 3, Scene 4

Hamlet visits the Queen privately, kills Polonius and confronts Gertrude with her sins.

Mother and son

This scene is often, in production, used to stress the oedipal tendency in Hamlet: the action is centred on the bed; gesture and inflection imply a frustrated sexual passion. It is too easy to fall into this interpretation of a scene that is actually set in Gertrude's 'closet': a private room, but not a bed-chamber. However, the theory of Hamlet's Oedipus complex is to be taken seriously: Sigmund Freud believed that Hamlet's irresolution in avenging his father comes from 'the obscure memory that he himself had contemplated the same deed against his father out of passion for his mother', an interesting explanation given the constant praise he heaps on his father. A disciple of Freud's, Ernest Jones, even published a full analysis of the play on the basis of the Oedipus complex.

The family

What is evident is that Hamlet's most important relationship with a woman is with his mother, not Ophelia: it is from her sins that he decides to condemn all womankind. The violent, out-of-control imagery of this scene conveys his disgust at the thought of her sinning. There is no need for a bed or passionate embraces to convey the power of the relationship. Essentially, Hamlet says one thing in this scene and says it repeatedly, but with much variety and heart-wringing imagery. It is this: 'Look at the difference between these two men. How could you choose Claudius?'

Hamlet

Examination

Examiner's tip

When writing on betrayal (question 2, page 75) you may well feel that the most emotionally draining betrayal for Hamlet was that of his mother, who betrayed both his dead father and himself. This scene is full of evidence that she too can be brought to see this betrayal as relating to herself as well as Claudius.

The tone moves from the bitterly accusatory, 'kill a king and marry with his brother', to the almost apologetic, 'I must be cruel only to be kind'. The accusation, incidentally, does not necessarily imply that Gertrude had a direct hand in the murder, as Hamlet sees the two events as one single crime. Hamlet may use pictures of the two kings, or the Ghost's reappearance may prompt him, or he may ask Gertrude to abstain from sex or insist on the opposite, but the imagery conveys the same meaning throughout.

You will find it helpful to make three lists of images here. First of all you could find images of the glory and goodness of Old Hamlet: the comparisons to Classical gods in lines 55–62 would be a good start. Then you could look for images of corruption, evil and sickness for Claudius: 'mildew'd ear' (of corn) or 'cutpurse of the empire'. Finally, you should make a similar list of terms that relate to the relationship between Gertrude and Claudius: there is a sickening sequence from line 184 onwards. The effect of

Corruption these images is to produce some repentance on the part of Gertrude, but no practical effect, the answer to her 'What shall I do?' being inconclusive. As for her attempt to 'tax him home', it never even got started.

The Ghost

There has been much speculation on the significance of the Ghost's appearance here. It speaks much less than on its previous appearance, simply reminding Hamlet of his 'almost blunted purpose' and of his promise not to harm his mother. It appears at a time when Hamlet's eloquence and disgust at Claudius are running away with him and Hamlet instantly knows what the Ghost is going to say. Does that (together with the fact that Gertrude cannot see the Ghost) mean that it is a creation of Hamlet's conscience and imagination? Probably not: Shakespeare is always adept at creating ghosts (Banquo's, for instance) which are both actual materialisations and reflections of conscience. The suggestion that the Queen cannot see the Ghost because she is guilty of his murder flies in the face of the evidence. Much more reasonable is to think

Hamlet that it appears to Hamlet alone because he is the object of its message and mission.

What does the murder of Polonius do for Hamlet's position in the power game with Claudius? It cannot aid his revelation of the guilt of Claudius: evident guilt of a crime today has more impact than putative guilt of a crime some months ago. Does it mean that he now has no defence against the King's plan to send him to England? Think about the wily schemes of Hamlet, Polonius and Claudius: the play, the concealment behind the arras and the visit to England. The first two schemes have had dramatic effects, but the proponents are now dead or under a death sentence. Only Claudius's England plot survives, but for how much longer?

■ Self-test questions Act 3

Who? Why? What? How? Where? When?
1 Who is 'in his retirement marvellous distempered'?
2 Why, according to Hamlet, does he not kill the King at prayer?
3 What is brief 'as woman's love'?
4 What is Claudius's assessment of Hamlet's mental and emotional state at the end of 3.1?
5 What prevents people committing suicide, according to Hamlet?
6 What is the reason for the Ghost's visit?
7 What is 'backed like a weasel'?
8 Where does Hamlet assert that Ophelia should go in 3.1?
9 Where does Polonius hide himself and meet his death?
10 When does the King rise and cause the play to be abandoned?

Complete the quotes
Find the following important quotations in Act 3, identify the speaker and complete the phrase or sentence.
1 'Almost as bad, good mother ...'
2 ''Sblood, do you think I am easier to be played on ...'
3 'To die, to sleep ...'
4 'Th'observed of all observers ...'
5 'O, my offence is rank, it smells to heaven ...'
6 'Thou turn'st my eyes ...'
7 'It was a brute part of him ...'
8 'There's something in his soul ...'
9 'My words fly up ...'
10 'You are the Queen ...'

The pangs of conscience
1 In what sense does 'conscience ... make cowards of us all' (3.1, line 83)?
2 What causes Hamlet to say, 'That's wormwood' (3.2, line 176) relating to his mother's conscience?
3 Why do the King's prayers (3.3) not go to Heaven? Is his sense of conscience real?
4 How does the Queen's conscience change her response to Hamlet's accusations?
5 In what two ways is the Ghost appealing to Hamlet's conscience?

Sexual disgust
'Frailty, thy name is woman' expressed Hamlet's opinion in Act 1, Scene 2. It is, however, repeated in much of his imagery in this act. See how many examples you can find. Also find examples of either obscene or disgusted references to the sexual act.

Act 4, Scenes 1–3

Hamlet is taken and despatched to England.

The intensity of the drama drops in Act 4. The first three scenes are narrative, with the sardonic and bitter humour of Hamlet to the fore. Scene 4 is largely emblematic, despite another major soliloquy. Scene 5 begins in pathetic mode with the madness of Ophelia, and it is only when Laertes breaks down the doors later in the scene that the tension again begins to build. By the end of the act the news of Hamlet's return and the multiple stratagems of the King and Laertes (the spirit of Polonius surviving him!) set up the final confrontations.

The King

The most fascinating feature of these three scenes is the presentation of the King, who is given many speeches in different settings, even soliloquy. His priorities, methods of deception and awareness of audience are never better illustrated.

The family

Claudius's first major speech, to Gertrude alone (4.1, lines 12–23) is frank about his instinct for self-preservation in two ways: Hamlet must be restrained before he attacks Claudius, and the King must also think of an excuse for not controlling Hamlet. Less frank is his comment on his motives for not doing so: 'so much was our love...'. Why should he be dishonest on this point? His speech to Rosencrantz and Guildenstern is both abrupt in its summons and flatteringly polite in style ('Friends', 'I pray you...', etc.) and by the beginning of Scene 3 he is presenting the public version of events to the court.

The court

Partly he is deceiving them: line 2 seems to be referring to a dangerous criminal whom Claudius has only just found out about, rather than a prince whose opposition to the usurper has been the subject of plot and counter-plot. Partly he is asking them to help him deceive the public: they must spread the word that Hamlet's departure is the result of a well-thought-out policy ('deliberate pause'). In his dialogue with Hamlet the King is not interested in engaging in wordplay and delivers the message of departure brusquely, with the reference to 'thine especial safety' being for the benefit of the court. Only in the final soliloquy can he express his real views. He is threatening England (lines 61–66 of Scene 3 are full of menace) into killing Hamlet to rid himself of 'the hectic in my blood'. The instability beneath the superficial control becomes more obvious.

Hamlet accepts his destiny

Hamlet

Hamlet, surprisingly, makes no attempt to argue against being sent to England. There are at least four possible reasons, all of which can be seen as true. He has no case, the murder being so obvious; his position would have been weakened by staying in Denmark when Polonius's death was to be investigated; he already has his plans for turning it to advantage; he now accepts what destiny has to offer. This last is the most interesting. Hamlet has plotted and planned, pretended madness, set up a play, and is no nearer achieving his end. When he returns from the aborted journey to England, he certainly feels himself in the hands of Fate. For all his thought, all five deaths he is responsible for (omitting Gertrude) come from taking opportunist advantage of the victim's own plot.

Tragedy

Coursework

'Not where he eats...' (Scene 3, line 19) onwards is an excellent summary of the somewhat fevered balance which Shakespeare maintains with Hamlet's wit. The joke about worms (the Diet of Worms was a council of religious leaders) is a neat pun, but the speech dwells on decay and corruption of the body, the transience of greatness and the death of kings.

Scenes 2 and 3 of Act 4 offer an opportunity to relish the sardonic, anarchic and somewhat unbalanced humour typical of Hamlet's 'antic disposition'. Let us find examples of three types of humour associated with Hamlet. He is incapable of speaking of Rosencrantz and Guildenstern without pouring scorn on their time-serving dishonesty. Compare the sponge image (4.2, lines 11–20) with the recorders in Act 3. Another element is morbid 'black' humour. Find all the references you can to worms and rotting bodies. This form of humour recurs in Act 5: the idea that 'a king may go a progress through the guts of a beggar' is similar to those expressed in the graveyard. Finally, we can derive most pleasure from the ways in which Hamlet simultaneously insults and perplexes Claudius. Lines 33–37 of Scene 3 are a perfect example, as is the father/mother confusion (think of 'uncle-father' and the early comments about kin and kind) followed by an exit at the double.

The family

Act 4, Scene 4

Fortinbras advances across Denmark en route to Poland.

This scene, except for the first 8 lines of Fortinbras and the Captain, is omitted in the Folio collection of Shakespeare's plays, and also in the Oxford Shakespeare edition. G R Hibbard, the editor, claims that it was cut originally because 'they do nothing to advance the action, nor do they reveal anything new about Hamlet and his state of mind.' This is largely true. The soliloquy is an elegant summary of things that have been expressed more vividly in the white heat of emotion. The presence of examples to shame him, the suspicion of cowardice, and so on are familiar, and the reference to 'a father kill'd', a mother stain'd' is probably the tamest expression of the incest/murder theme.

The scene, however, is not without purpose. Structurally the departure of Hamlet needs to be separated from the madness of Ophelia, which must occur much later as Laertes has time to return from Paris. Eight lines would hardly serve to create the right dramatic impression.

The avenging sons

The most important purpose of the scene, however, is to amplify the theme of vengeance and honour. Laertes and Fortinbras, even Pyrrhus to an extent, are examples of dynamic avengers who serve as a commentary on Hamlet.

Revenge

The results of that commentary are challenging. Hamlet, we acknowledge, should take more dynamic action to avenge his father and Fortinbras, in particular, provides an ideal example for him: or does he? The corrupting effect the pursuit of vengeance has on Laertes is obvious, but in Fortinbras's case it is equally harmful. Discovered in his attempt at vengeance and distracted into an attack on Poland, he prepares to risk thousands of troops in an attack on a place of no worth. If this is unthinking honour, does not Hamlet's over-thoughtful indecision have something to recommend it?

Examiner's tip

Examination

The theme of revenge (question 1, page 73) is obviously central to the play, and equally obviously Fortinbras is a contrast to Hamlet. Young Fortinbras, 'holding a weak supposal' of Denmark's strength, proposed to regain lands lost. He is equally happy invading a small patch of Poland. What can you deduce of his original motivation?

Hamlet's reaction to another example is another vow to try harder: 'My thoughts be bloody or be nothing worth.' Do his future actions suggest an increased ruthlessness, or is the future bloodshed as unpremeditated as the killing of Polonius?

Act 4, Scene 5

The madness of Ophelia and the return of Laertes.

Hamlet without the Prince

For the only time in the play attention moves away from Hamlet. Even in the two scenes in Act 1 where he does not appear, he is a principal topic of conversation.

The family

Now, although Hamlet's actions lie behind current events and Laertes' plans of revenge, Act 4, Scenes 5 and 7 are dominated by the children of Polonius, with Hamlet represented by messages in the very short Scene 6 and in Scene 7. All these scenes contain a large number of anonymous characters, plus Horatio in a very surprising role of adviser to the Queen. The presence of these characters is caused partly by the number of messages sent and delivered, but even more so by the dismantling of the court with the three deaths (two as yet unknown by the King).

Scene 5 is layered in short sections on the following themes: exposition (lines 1–20, 75–110), the madness of Ophelia (lines 21–74, 152–197) and the wrath of Laertes (lines 111–152, 198–216).

Events, until now, have risen from the original situation in a flowing sequence. Now we need to be told of events that have changed the situation since Hamlet killed Polonius and was banished. Thus, there are two 'messenger' speeches providing virtually uninterrupted direct exposition. The

Revenge

Gentleman tells of Ophelia's madness at the beginning and, in the second expository phase, a messenger tells of the assault of Laertes. There is a dramatic formality about the speech, with the opening metaphor of the ocean and such phrases as 'antiquity forgot'. This resembles, to some extent, the messenger speeches of Greek tragedy, where all major action occurred off-stage. Claudius's speech to Gertrude (lines 75 onwards) is also a part of the expository section in the middle of the scene, summarising the sorrows that 'come not single spies,/But in battalions.'

The madness of Ophelia

Madness

What does the madness of Ophelia mean? There are two elements in what she says or sings: the meaning of the snatches of songs and the meaning of flowers. There is also a further meaning in the response of the onlookers: even the King is sufficiently distracted from self-justification and self-preservation to add to the pathos. Laertes, between expressions of grief, is further stirred to thoughts of revenge and specifically compares Ophelia's situation to that of their father: 'a young maid's wits' and 'an old man's life'. The scene is obviously a further stage in the theme of madness, but it should also be seen as a conventional (and, in this case, very moving) dramatic device.

If we examine the songs, we find recollections of well-known ballads, notably *Walsingham* where the loved one is a pilgrim to the shrine of Walsingham: hence the cockle hat and sandals worn by a pilgrim. It is a mistake to think that every word can be applied with precision to Ophelia's griefs:

Corruption

after all, Shakespeare is quoting existing songs. Examine Ophelia's snatches of ballads and see how far you can apply them to two general themes: unhappiness in love and death of someone beloved (not necessarily a sweetheart). You will find Ophelia in her madness mourning her father and her loss of Hamlet's love. You will also occasionally find (the snatch beginning 'By Gis and by Saint Charity' in particular) a coarseness that is unexpected in Ophelia and echoes Hamlet at the play.

The flowers all have a poignant symbolism which we are encouraged to bear in mind, by Ophelia pointing it out in the case of rosemary (remembrance) and pansies (thoughts). Five flowers are presented, those two plus fennel and columbines (both suggesting marital infidelity) and rue or herb of grace (repentance). Which of the three characters do you think each flower is presented to? She has a daisy (unhappy love) for herself and the violets (faithfulness) withered with her father's death.

The wrath of Laertes

Revenge

Laertes appears as the traditional avenger, but falls easy prey to Claudius's coolness and cunning. Laertes storms in with his followers, who are immediately dismissed, and confronts the King with the sort of language that Hamlet has used in previous curses. In saying that remaining calm shows him to be no son of Polonius he uses imagery of sexual corruption. His next major speech begins in terms more reminiscent of Lucianus in *The Murder of Gonzago*: blackness and hell are everywhere. From this threatening start, note how quickly he is subdued. The King asks one logical question and Laertes calms down – by the end of the scene Claudius is confident that he has an ally. In seeking vengeance, perhaps too little thought is as dangerous as too much.

The court

You should examine the reactions to Laertes of both King and Queen. Gertrude says little, but all on one theme and revealing about her attitude to her husband. As for Claudius, he has to face a situation where the messenger begs him, 'Save yourself' (by flight, presumably); how does he cope with it?

Coursework

The court

In Act 1, Scene 2, the opening stage direction mentions Claudius's Council, the Ambassadors and 'Others' apart from the prominent characters. Act 4, Scene 5 mentions Horatio and 'a Gentleman'. We are clearly meant to see Claudius in isolation and possibly in decline. Laertes will find no reduction in his skills in manipulating others, however.

Act 4, Scenes 6 and 7

Hamlet's story; the plot of Claudius and Laertes; the death of Ophelia.

Shakespeare does little to develop Hamlet's story in Scene 6: we have a graphic account in Act 5, Scene 2, and to anticipate too much would spoil that narrative. Scene 6 imparts the essential news and also provides a pause in which Claudius can be imagined persuading Laertes of his innocence and Hamlet's guilt. By the time we rejoin them in Scene 7, the King has already convinced Laertes of everything except why he took no action against Hamlet.

The family

The reasons he gives reflect his manipulation of the truth: the Queen loves Hamlet and he loves the Queen so much that he could not bear to do anything, and the common people would have risen in support of Hamlet. If neither of these reasons is absolutely untrue, neither suggests the depth of Claudius's villainy, though the weakness implied makes it sound convincing. However, he has done something about it, something which he thinks is successful until Hamlet's message (lines 42–45). Why does he not mention this to Laertes?

The King manipulates Laertes

The King's ability to manipulate a situation moves him from calming down Laertes (in the expectation that they will hear later of Hamlet's death) to using him as an agent of that death.

Revenge

Laertes is full of protestations of revenge: 'But my revenge will come', 'Thus diest thou.' The King sets up an attractive scenario (killing Hamlet without blame) and he has Laertes' agreement to be ruled by him. Then he keeps the fury simmering while telling a tale in leisurely polished verse about Lamord, appealing to Laertes' rather sententious code of chivalry, with little reference to Hamlet (though you will note the anticipatory allusion, 'Did Hamlet so envenom'). Suddenly, from this, he moves on to urgent questions ('Laertes, was your father dear to you?' 'what would you undertake...?') which render Laertes helpless to do other than co-operate with Claudius.

The court

You will appreciate the irony of 'To cut his throat i'th' church' (something Hamlet could not do) and the King's sanctimonious reply. From courtly narrative and stern questioning, the scene moves inevitably to brisk plotting. After Laertes' commitment three speeches follow, each one discussing a way to kill Hamlet – two ways too many as, with delicious irony, the conspirators find out.

The comparison between Hamlet and Laertes at this stage is again relevant. Laertes talks pompously of codes of honour and Hamlet, in Act 5, Scene 2, speaks respectfully of him more than once, so there is a temptation to see him as an ideal of chivalry (until temporarily corrupted by Claudius) and a model for Hamlet. Ask yourself therefore: which one is (on his enemy's admission) 'most generous and free from all contriving' and which one buys poisons from mountebanks (quack salesmen)?

Hamlet

Examiner's tip

Laertes' behaviour here is near to that of the traditional avenger (see question 1, page 73). Not only is he intent on killing, but he has armed himself with a poison (to kill Claudius?). Less the 'very noble youth' of Hamlet's description than the image of Machiavellian murderer, he nevertheless fails to carry through his revenge as planned.

Examination

'There is a willow…'

The finest of the 'messenger' speeches ends the act, with Gertrude speaking outside her character, though not contradicting it: her affection for Ophelia is several times expressed, though never leading to positive action.

After the simple announcement, 'Your sister's drown'd, Laertes', the speech begins formally with the natural description setting the scene. The reference both creates an appropriate scene and has a symbolic purpose: willows suggest sadness, as in many other references in Shakespeare and elsewhere. So it proceeds throughout the speech: Ophelia drowning amid a medley of flowers is visually appealing and appropriate to her character. Imagery of plants and flowers has been common in the play: Hamlet describes the world as an 'unweeded garden' in his very first soliloquy. So Ophelia dies in a romantic and beautiful scene beloved of painters, but also with a garland of flowers which symbolise unhappy love, death, etc. 'Dead men's fingers' indeed symbolise death and, under their 'grosser name', sexual love.

There are many subtle features of the speech that are worth close attention. The natural scene becomes an active participant in the events. An 'envious sliver' caused her death, a pretty personification which also avoids the question of suicide, deliberately never resolved, though discussed in the next scene.

The 'weeping brook' is an example of the pathetic fallacy which is the device by which nature is presented as sharing the emotions of the human protagonist. Personification extends to her garments that try to save her until they become 'too heavy with their drink'. The identification of Ophelia with her natural surroundings is also emphasised: see what examples you can find.

Madness

Finally, what sort of madness does Ophelia suffer from? Her death seems a natural consequence of how we last saw her: barely aware of her surroundings and her situation, making garlands of flowers, singing old songs: the fact that ballads have been replaced by hymns ('lauds') is probably of no significance. Compared with Hamlet's assumed madness, this is passive and pathetic, a regression from the present.

Act 5, Scene 1

The graveyard: jokes and songs, Yorick's skull and Ophelia's funeral.

Intimations of mortality: the Prince and the clowns

Throughout *Hamlet* there is a preoccupation with death: the action begins with the ghost of a murdered man asking his son to avenge him, a son who regularly considers the merits of suicide. But the preoccupation is not merely with death itself, but with a debate on the value of life, whether the ambitions, affectations and joys of life are outweighed by the sufferings and rendered pointless by the fact of death. Hamlet is welcomed back to Danish soil by a sort of symposium on death: the Gravediggers use Ophelia's burial for jests and debate; Hamlet provides a commentary on life and death inspired by the Gravedigger's songs in the grave – gravedigger and prince come together in a uneasy mix of humour and philosophy; Ophelia's funeral is marked by violent confrontation between Laertes and Hamlet. What is worth noting is that the 'serious' action of the scene occupies only some 80-plus lines after over 200 lines in which jests, puns and riddles are never far away.

Coursework

Tragedy
There is much material throughout the play for the essay on page 70, but more in Act 5 than anywhere else. You need to consider the contribution of the gravediggers to the macabre sense of death, of Osric to the sense of emptiness at court and in building tension towards the duel, both in scenes that are very funny just before the climax of the tragedy.

The remarkable quality of this scene is the double power of this graveside humour: the fusion of macabre humour and forceful commentary on the transience of life becomes more shocking the funnier it is.

The Gravedigger's humour is typical of many Shakespearean clowns. What is not typical is the subject of the humour: suicide, executions and the rotting of dead bodies; and his neglectful cheerfulness which is, in itself, a commentary

Corruption

on the unimportance of human life. Feste, a professional jester in *Twelfth Night*, calls himself a 'corrupter of words', and this is a large part of clowns' humour, though one may assume that Shakespeare intends errors like 'Se offendendo' (for 'se defendendo', in self-defence) to be seen as mistakes, not deliberate jokes. See what other examples of the comic misuse of words you can find.

Another element in the humour is the parody or burlesque of learning. This is seen best in the Gravedigger's disquisition on suicide. You will find several examples, such as the portentous statement that 'an act hath three branches', based on a defence counsel's argument in an actual suicide case, but in this case all the branches are identical. The repeated 'argal' is a neat example of both the affectation of learning and the misuse of words, being an attempt at 'ergo', Latin for 'therefore'. This use of 'therefore' also reflects the pseudo-logic employed by Shakespearean clowns. This is shown by the accurate, but infuriatingly literal, answers made by the Gravedigger to Hamlet, as in the sequence on whose grave it is (lines 115–132). See what other examples you can discover. This sequence also throws up typical wordplay with the puns on 'lie', with the extra sense of 'untruth'.

Finally, clowns specialise in songs and riddles. The songs are very evident here, their subject matter all too relevant, and the Gravedigger takes advantage of his slow-witted companion in the riddle of the strongest builder. The macabre is never far away even when the humour is at its silliest: as the simple stooge puzzles and ends up with 'Mass, I cannot tell', the message comes through of the power of the gallows and the grave.

Hamlet

Though framed in a more intellectual way, Hamlet's reflections from a distance chime in with the Gravedigger's world-view, and eventually their conversational strands meet harmoniously with talk of Yorick and the best preserved corpses. Hamlet's theme is mutability and the transitory nature of human life, wealth and power affording no protection. Note Hamlet's choice of imaginary people behind the skulls thrown up by the Gravedigger. It is obviously not an exact commentary on the events at court: the longest passage is about a lawyer, with a shocking juxtaposition of his 'quiddities' and 'quillities' and a 'mad knave' knocking him 'about the sconce with a dirty shovel.' However, you should be able to recognise certain references. The passing comment about Cain takes us back to the King at prayer. The politician and the fawning courtier remind us of the three enemies whose deaths Hamlet has already caused and 'my Lady Worm' is not unconnected with Hamlet's obsession with the 'frailty' of women.

The court

Remarkably, this set piece of macabre comedy has an increasingly realistic edge. Note the way in which the Gravedigger dates his years in the job or Hamlet reminisces about life at court (when he was seven years old or less, according to Shakespeare's dates).

Corruption

The remains under discussion move from those belonging to figures of Hamlet's imagination to real people: Yorick (whose skull inspires Hamlet's most famously morbid gesture), or a tanner whose body will last because it is tanned already, or the possessors of 'pocky corses' which nearly fall apart at the interment – something is literally rotten in Denmark!

Hamlet's morbid preoccupation with death and the decay of the body surfaces often in the play, sometimes in combination with a sardonic sense of the absurd. Look back to Act 4, Scene 3, for good examples. Here, in

Hamlet

fascinated disgust, Hamlet traces the progress of the great (Alexander and Caesar) after death, even giving Caesar a silly little rhyme that a jester might be proud of. Think about what this fascination tells us about Hamlet and his views not just of death, but of Fate and human greatness: what does it say, for instance, about his attitude to securing the Crown at all costs?

The funeral

In totally different style from the first part of the scene, the funeral takes full advantage of the same inspired piece of staging: the open grave before us, with the bodies both of the long-buried and the newly dead. The grave is never the background to the action, always the focal point of it. The Gravedigger and his mate work, sing and joke there; Hamlet kneels by it (or bends over it) examining its contents; Ophelia is placed there; the Queen strews flowers in it; in turn, Laertes and Hamlet leap into it and then fight. It is a remarkably bold piece of stagecraft. That apart, this section of the scene reads somewhat uneasily; in performance, the audience is too swept away by the drama to question it.

There are some odd reactions. Hamlet's explanation to Horatio of who Laertes is seems mainly to serve the purpose of removing any sense of enmity on Hamlet's part ('a very noble youth'). The return of Hamlet inspires surprisingly little comment: though the King has been warned that he will 'beg leave to see your kingly eyes', his appearance roaring a war cry at Ophelia's funeral is not what one would expect. The argument between Laertes and the Priest may seem unnecessary, but has a precise dramatic function. Shakespeare is at pains to make Ophelia's death ambiguous (an apparent suicide rather than a proven one) and this halfway stage between unsanctified ground and full rites is perfect. Without the full ceremonial there is still plenty of opportunity to stress Ophelia's virgin purity: once again the imagery of flowers is used, notably in Laertes' reference to violets springing from 'her fair and unpolluted flesh'.

Most difficult to assess is Hamlet's behaviour. There is enough evidence in Laertes' entry in Act 4, Scene 5, for us to accept his flamboyant expressions and gestures of grief as in character: note the Classical comparisons and the numerical hyperbole ('ten times treble'). But Hamlet's behaviour up till now has not prepared us for his reaction, with its absurd list of the awful tasks ('eat a crocodile'!) he would perform for Ophelia and his out-doing of Laertes in imagery of mountains (Pelion and Ossa were neighbouring mountains in Greek myth).

Hamlet

Why does he behave so? There is no need to do it to provide a reason for the fencing match, which is an apparently friendly affair already set up by Claudius. Hamlet is changed by his return, apparently more fatalistic than before, but also aware that his discovery of the mission of Rosencrantz and Guildenstern opens up the struggle between himself and Claudius, so 'This is I,/Hamlet the Dane' does not just mean that he is Danish, but that he is 'Denmark', the King. Then we must realise that he is unaware till now of Ophelia's death. The dramatic irony of his enquiries about the identity of the corpse to be buried is highly effective for an audience in the know and his explosion of enraged grief is understandable. The way he responds to Laertes is debatable: is it caused by feelings of rivalry or is he, perhaps, attempting to show up Laertes' undignified actions by taking them one stage further?

The court

However, the real question concerns Hamlet's feelings about Ophelia. In the play the intensity of love conveyed by the 'forty thousand brothers' speech (more numerical hyperbole) has not been seen. The answer, probably, is that *Hamlet* has a solid hinterland behind the play itself. We are often invited to imagine life before the murder in the orchard destroyed all sense of normality. Just like Gertrude's reference to her wish for Ophelia to have married Hamlet, the devotion of which Hamlet speaks belongs to this earlier time.

The family

Act 5, Scene 2

The climax: four deaths and the election of Fortinbras as King.

A leisurely approach to death

As with the previous scene, Shakespeare's approach to imminent tragedy shows astonishing confidence in his dramatic skills. In Scene 1, a new comic character (two, if you count his straightman) was introduced and given more on-stage time than Ophelia's funeral. In Scene 2, almost incredibly, the same thing happens again. The entry of the King occurs over halfway through the scene and within less than 120 lines only Horatio and the dying Hamlet remain alive of main characters. Before that, however, Hamlet has told in leisurely style the story of changing the royal commission, and Osric has been given a lengthy opportunity (100 lines) to show off his foolishness in his one appearance in the play. Yet for all this, tension is by no means reduced.

You might like to think for yourself why Shakespeare introduces these one-scene characters so late in the play and why comedy plays around the edges of the wholesale slaughter that ends the play. One thing to bear in mind is that, so long as Polonius and Rosencrantz and Guildenstern were alive, Hamlet was never short of material on which to sharpen his wit. Perhaps you might think that enough preparation has gone into these events in Act 4, and that scenes involving Claudius and Laertes would be redundant. Whatever you think, do not simply assume that 'comic relief' is the answer: these scenes do not relieve the tragedy so much as intensify it.

Hamlet

How is Hamlet changed on his return? The narrative of the royal commission, well told in generally regular blank verse, suggests some self-control. Odd lines like 'With ho! such bugs and goblins in my life' suggest Hamlet's contempt for Claudius and love of ridicule, and his version with the repetition of 'as' is a neat parody of diplomatic jargon, but it is, in the main, a steady account by Hamlet's standards. What does he feel about causing the deaths of Rosencrantz and Guildenstern? Is his view of them changed or the same? He summons up some fury and disgust at the King, and a line like 'He that hath kill'd my king and whor'd my mother' sums up much of what drives Hamlet on to vengeance. Have previous expressions of the view been similar, or more violent, or expressed with more variety of imagery?

The family

Of interest here is one of the few specific references to Hamlet's desire to be king. So intense is his agony at the murder/marriage that his own hopes are rarely expressed, but we learn that Claudius 'popp'd in' (a suitably inglorious phrase) to seize the Crown that he felt was his. You should note that the practice of 'elected monarchy' was common in medieval times: the accession of eldest son was not automatic.

What can we learn about Hamlet's current state of mind from the line, 'There's a divinity that shapes our ends'? How is that reflected later in the scene (lines 170–175) when he calmly accepts the proposition of a friendly duel, despite what he knows of the King's intentions towards him and Laertes' probable enmity? Look at the lines beginning, 'We defy augury' (lines 215–220), expressing Hamlet's new-found fatalism.

Once again Hamlet is seen as the enemy of affectation, the opposite of the courtier. The humour surrounding Osric works in various, slightly different ways. His speech in itself is comical. Shakespeare parodies with relish the Euphuistic style, an affected manner of speech derived from Thomas Lyly's very

popular prose work, *Euphues*, and the elaborate speech is seconded by equally
foppish gesture. The humour is then extended by Hamlet's imitation and,

finally, by Osric's inability to understand the imitation of his
own style. However, you might find most interest in the hat
incident (lines 93 onwards). The humour derives from Osric's
fanciful gestures with his 'bonnet', but continues with the
courtier hopelessly confused by Hamlet's change of mind about
the temperature. If, like a good courtier, he must agree with
the prince, what is he to say? What earlier discussion are you reminded of?

The court

The purpose of Osric's appearance is an ever-interesting topic
for speculation. Apart from other uses, it extends the criticism
of court life beyond Claudius's political scheming. Usually we
have seen the court carrying out business, reflecting the will
of the King. In relaxed mode, all it can produce is this foolish 'waterfly'.

Coursework

The complicated wager (terms so complicated as to seem self-contradictory)
is typical of Osric, but the final confrontation is now set up. Contrast Hamlet's
easy manner with the chivalric 'honour' of Laertes when he enters: he cannot
be reconciled before advised thus by 'some elder masters of honour'. Hamlet's
view of such honour is well illustrated by his comment when invited by
Osric to 'vouchsafe the answer'. In codes of honour 'answer' means to accept
the challenge; Hamlet debunks the whole thing with 'How if I
answer no?'

Forgiveness and malice

It is remarkable that the scene of the assembled court begins so normally. The

courtiers know that Hamlet has been sent to England because
he is mad: at least we presume they do, since the Gravedigger
does. However, they gather round prepared to applaud the
skill and the entertainment, not questioning his return or his
sanity. Laertes knows he is about to attempt to kill Hamlet
ingloriously, yet he discourses on honour like the noble young
gentleman he is reputed to be. The King knows all that there is to be known
about evil past, present and to come, but he plays the part of a benign monarch
enforcing reconciliation of the two young men. And, as for Hamlet, he is not
deceived about his uncle, though he unwisely trusts Laertes, and faces what
is to come with generous confession and disarming modesty. (For once,
Hamlet is not strictly honest: he has told Horatio he expects to win, though
how he has been able to remain in 'continual practice' is a mystery.)

Hamlet's speech to Laertes (lines 222–240) is a poised and polished apology, well reasoned with questions and answers, placing the blame on his madness and greeting Laertes as his 'brother'. You will find that this is not the last time Hamlet refers to Laertes in this way. This is Hamlet in untypically courtly and diplomatic mode: why do you think he takes such pains to establish his bond of brotherhood with Laertes?

The family

Death by sword and poison

In some ways we return to the beginning. The King will drink to Hamlet and, when he drinks, the trumpets and kettle drums will sound: the Danish celebration that Hamlet found 'more honour'd in the breach than the observance' in Act 1. The 'smiling villain' is with us again, honouring Hamlet with his wager, throwing the 'union' in the cup and, with an ironical 'Here's to thy health', attempting to persuade him to drink.

Examiner's tip

Examination

In both the titles under consideration on pages 73 and 75 the final scene is of great importance. In considering the theme of revenge (question 1) it is wonderfully ironic that so much planning of revenge ends in risk and uncertainty. Is it for this that Hamlet set up a play, or the King sent Hamlet to England, or Laertes produced an infallible poison?

In any contest like this duel, there is suspense: who will win and how? Here it is intensified by the poisoned 'unbated' sword, of course, and especially by the poisoned cup – a more random killer not dependent on the progress of the contest. It is dramatically essential for Hamlet to win the early bouts: what reasons can you think of for this?

The dishonour of Claudius and Laertes in the fencing match goes beyond their initial dishonour in preparing for Hamlet's death. The King is warned that Gertrude is about to drink, but fails to stop her: 'do not drink', he says, ineffectually. Think what else he could have said which would have prevented her, and why he does not say it. Laertes becomes impatient to end the duel and, not prepared to wait, stabs Hamlet in a break in the fighting; his comment that it is almost against his conscience is no excuse for such a shameful act.

Examiner's tip

Examination

Question 2, page 75, needs equal attention to this last scene. Betrayal, in every sense of the word, is all around in the duel scene. Laertes betrays Hamlet, for instance, but his betrayal of himself is more comprehensive: he betrays his honour, his good name, his sense of self, but also, in practical terms, he betrays himself to death.

The deaths occur on a cumulative basis. Hamlet's success causes both Gertrude's celebratory drink and Laertes' illicit strike. Then 'they change rapiers'. This poses a big question for a stage director: does Hamlet, aware of the deception, force the sword from Laertes' hand and deliberately take the 'unbated' weapon? Maybe so, but he is aware only of the lack of a protective tip and responds in natural anger to wound Laertes. It is only with Claudius that he deliberately, if belatedly, kills in revenge. It is ironic that, given that Hamlet's killing has always been opportunist, the King creates the opportunity for his own death.

The timing of the deaths is superbly handled. The Queen is doomed

before most people are aware of it, so, as Laertes and Hamlet wound each other, her death occurs seemingly unprompted. The King, the only one actually stabbed to death, expires rapidly and violently, while Laertes lives long enough to ask Hamlet for forgiveness and Hamlet, the least wounded with

Revenge

perhaps less poison in his blood, is the last to die, with an appropriate focus on him.

The final minutes of the play are an appropriate reminder that Hamlet is a

noble prince, brave and capable in the arts of war, possessing regal authority. One of the problems with the character as a tragic hero is that throughout the play we see him only in his afflicted state, and it takes imagination to conceive of him as the prince much loved by the people, and the 'expectancy and

Hamlet

rose of the fair state' whom Ophelia remembered. In his last scene his assault on the King crying 'thou incestuous, murd'rous, damned Dane' is in the style to which we are accustomed, his sudden attack reminiscent of that on Polonius, though more fully justified. However, for the most part, from outfacing Laertes both in fencing skills and nobility of character, Hamlet appears in heroic vein here. He even manages a sort of forgiveness for Laertes whose behaviour here is contemptible, though, of course, he has Laertes' father on his conscience. Consider the part played, in our final impressions of Hamlet, by his concern that his story should be told justly, his care to preserve Horatio's life, his royal responsibility in nominating Fortinbras as King, Horatio's words at his death and Fortinbras's last speech. The evocative last words, 'the rest is silence', combine with Horatio's response to his death in creating a romantic mood that is extremely moving, even if the concept of 'sweet prince' tended to produce, at one time, unduly sentimental interpretations of the character of Hamlet.

Normality returns

Shakespeare himself leaves no time for sentiment over Hamlet's death: no sooner has Horatio asked 'flights of angels' to 'sing thee to thy rest' than the drums sound and Fortinbras's army enters with English ambassadors seeking praise from Claudius for killing Rosencrantz and Guildenstern, the last rites of the crazy passage of events that has just ended with a final death toll of eight.

The progress to normality at the end of a Shakespearean tragedy doubtless has something to do with the practicalities of dealing with the dead on a stage with no curtain: somebody has to remove the bodies, which also invites the possibility of someone taking charge and the inevitability of some sort of sober ceremonial. However, the use made of this by Shakespeare goes well beyond practicalities. In the cases of many Shakespearean tragic heroes, most especially Hamlet, we see the world through their eyes and experiences; the conclusion places them within a larger world which goes on, more or less successfully, though the Danish court has nearly consigned itself to oblivion.

The return to normality is signalled in various ways. One is to emphasise that what has occurred is profoundly abnormal. Fortinbras, in his opening and closing statements, suggests that the scene is suitable to the hunt or the battlefield, not the court. Horatio sums up what we have been watching admirably in the list beginning 'carnal, bloody and unnatural acts'. If this has all been unnatural, what is natural? A new responsible king takes over: he has a claim ('some rights of memory') because, for large periods of time in the Middle Ages and later, Denmark and Norway were united in one kingdom. This responsible king honours the dead Hamlet and restores order, with proper ceremonial and soldiers firing a peal of ordnance.

This is how things should be. It is only afterwards that we appreciate the irony of the Prince of Norway taking the Danish throne. After all, this is the consequence of the final working out of the story of two Danish kings who in turn, by force of arms and force of diplomacy, subdued two successive Kings of Norway to their will. There is, in *Hamlet*, an overwhelming sense of waste of which this political suicide is a part.

Revenge

■ Self-test questions Acts 4 and 5

Who? Why? What? How? Where? When?
1 Who referees the final fencing bout?
2 Who is Lamord?
3 Who describes whom as 'an absolute gentleman, full of most excellent differences'?
4 Why does Laertes quarrel with the Priest?
5 Why is the Ambassadors' expectation of thanks doubly doomed to failure?
6 What else happened on the day Hamlet was born?

7   What does Ophelia say happened to the violets?
8   How does Hamlet inform Horatio of his survival and return?
9   Where can Claudius look for the body of Polonius himself, according to Hamlet?
10 When does Gertrude drink the poison?

Complete the quotes

Find the following important quotations from Acts 4 and 5, identify the speaker and complete the phrase or sentence.

1   'There is a willow ...'
2   'But I cannot choose but weep ...'
3   'For he was likely, had he been put on ...'
4   'I am more an antique Roman ...'
5   'I knew him, Horatio ...'
6   'Imperious Caesar, dead and turn'd to clay ...'
7   'I thought thy bride-bed to have deck'd ...'
8   'Do it, England ...'
9   'Now get you to my lady's chamber ...'
10 'But I do prophesy ...'

The fact of death

Find and explain images of death in:

1   Hamlet's account of Polonius's whereabouts in 4.3;
2   Hamlet's discussion with the Captain in 4.4;
3   The songs of Ophelia in 4.5;
4   Gertrude's account of the death of Ophelia in 4.7;
5   The Gravedigger's comedy in 5.1;
6   Hamlet's discussion with the Gravedigger in 5.1;
7   The deaths of Claudius and Laertes in 5.2;
8   Hamlet's view of death in 5.2.

Extras

New characters who appear only in Acts 4 and 5 are Fortinbras, the Captain, the Sailors, various court servants, two gravediggers and Osric. In a few words each, try to summarise what they contribute to the play.

■ How to write a coursework essay

Different examining boards have different requirements for A Level coursework, but there are certain principles that hold good in every case. We will consider these and also two possible titles for coursework. However, essays can not only be of *different lengths*, but of *different types*. You are probably most likely to find yourself writing on one text (approximately 1,500–2,000 words), comparing two texts (3,000 words) or writing about a literary genre referring to at least three texts (up to 5,000 words). Most of these word-length requirements are optional maximums; *it is essential that you check with your teacher that there is no penalty for extra length.*

If you are choosing a comparative title, you must make sure that comparisons are made throughout, not necessarily in the same sentence, but at least in adjacent paragraphs. Your essay title must direct you to some specific comparison, not just a generalised survey of similarities and differences. Remember also that 'comparison' always implies 'contrast' as well – discussing different ways of approaching a theme, plot-line or genre can always be productive.

The single-text coursework essay is in many ways similar. A specific task is again essential, and once again your theme or line of argument must be kept before the reader throughout. Narration is almost always unhelpful: even at A Level, 'telling the story' is the most common failing. Almost equally dangerous is taking opinions from critics without fully understanding them and failing to absorb them into your arguments. *Copying* from critics without acknowledgement is, of course, plagiarism and can result in disqualification.

The need for a developing argument or comparison has implications for your method of approaching the essay. You should make general notes on the material (textual evidence, useful quotations, comments by critics, etc.), then shape them into an ordered framework (probably simply by numbering them in an appropriate order) before working through at least two or three drafts of the essay. You should be fully aware of what each paragraph is to be about, as far as possible signalling this to the reader in the first sentence, often called the *topic sentence* for this reason. With comparatively short essays like these, you should make sure that your style is concise and time is not wasted on unnecessary quotations. Relevant, fairly brief quotations are very valuable, absorbed into your sentences if very short, or set out on separate lines if slightly longer. It is unlikely that quotations of more than a few lines will really help you.

The actual presentation of your essay is also important. With coursework it is sheer carelessness to make errors in spelling, punctuation or syntax or (worst of all) to confuse or misspell characters' names. Unless there is a definite reason for doing otherwise, avoid slang and colloquialisms, including contractions like 'they've' for 'they have'.

The format of introduction–essay–conclusion is perfectly acceptable but, used over-formally, can weight the essay too much in the direction of semi-relevant generalisation at the beginning and the end. In a good essay, the conclusion will simply be the final stage of a developed argument.

Each of the example titles given below can be easily adapted to a comparative essay with another text(s). Use the outlines to form your notes on this text. The points should also help you to focus your approach to the other text(s).

An *outline* of a model answer has been supplied for each essay title below. Use this outline in conjunction with material in the **Who's who**, **Themes and images** and **Text commentary** sections of this guide. In addition, the points raised as **Examiner's tips** throughout the Text commentary should prove particularly useful.

The court

How convincing do you find Shakespeare's presentation of the court at Elsinore, in terms of politics, manners and characterisation?

It is probable that you will use your study of *Hamlet* for an examination question, rather than a coursework piece but, if you have the opportunity for a coursework essay, it might be pleasing to take a slightly oblique view, such as this, of the play, rather than tackling an obvious title like Hamlet's character (see **Who's who**) or the theme of revenge (see **Themes and images** and **How to write an examination essay**).

The first stage is to make clear in what terms you are judging the court to be convincing or not. The original tale of Amleth was set in the medieval Viking times, but Shakespeare does not wish to reproduce this. He would have been familiar with details of life in the sixteenth-century court at Kronborg Castle, Elsinore (Helsingor). Several English performers were in King Christian IV's company of actors, including Will Kempe, long-time Clown with Shakespeare's company, and it is a Renaissance-type court he is portraying. Not that the Danish element is strictly enforced: names are Italian and Latin as well as authentically Danish, and the troupe of actors appears to have come from London.

The world of politics is presented vividly and accurately. Give detailed accounts of Claudius's skill in public utterance, Polonius's one-man secret service (spying was an important feature of Queen Elizabeth I's Court) and the election of Kings. The ceremonial is also convincingly created: the public meetings, the forms of address, the repeated acknowledgement of the King's sole power. As for manners, you can study courtly politeness, devious 'economy with the truth' or the affectations of Osric. The court is furthermore revealed as a place for entertainment: plays, duels and drinking bouts (plus, one imagines, a successor to Yorick as jester).

All these deserve thorough treatment, but the characters provide the most important element in the creation of convincing court scenes. Perhaps the most significant is Polonius: he is an ally of the King who has not secured his position by birth or by generalship, but by rising in the Royal Household. He is Lord Chamberlain or a Privy Counsellor, and his approach to every problem is via the by-ways of spying and negotiation, not frontal physical attack. Claudius, too, is a King who operates within court, not on the battlefield; a King of deception, rhetoric and secret crimes, who has to be protected from the world by his Swiss Guards. The problems of the Danish Royal Family are exactly that: the problems that arise within the public halls and privy chambers of the palace, not to mention in the orchard. The range of court characters can be developed much further: take note of characters like Rosencrantz, Guildenstern and Osric whose ways of life depend on the King's smile or the fashion of the court.

A good conclusion would be to consider how the presentation of court life affects the tragedy. You should take note of how claustrophobic the tragedy becomes: no opening out on to battlefields or street brawls or triumphal marches. Except for some moments in Act 4 and, to an extent, the funeral of Ophelia, all the action is in the castle: even the corridors, stairs and lobbies are part of the tragic scene.

Tragedy

'Though Hamlet *is Shakespeare's most famous and most popular tragedy, the tragic action is constantly disturbed by comedy or irrelevance and the protagonist is inadequate as a tragic hero.' Do you find this a fair comment on the play?*

This is the sort of title that it is interesting to speculate on for coursework: it would probably be unfair to expect a candidate to think through such a complex title in the limited time of an examination. The first point to be made about preparing the essay is that there is no 'right' answer (you genuinely have to come to your own conclusion), but there are certain areas that must be covered.

Obviously you will have no trouble making the case that there are many scenes that are not strictly relevant to the main plot or the Polonius family sub-plot: think of scenes with the Players or the Gravediggers or Osric, for instance. Nor is it difficult to find humour amid the tragedy, from the Clown scene (Act 5, Scene 1) to Hamlet's satires on hypocrisy, foolishness and affectation. To this extent you must agree with the quotation: the debatable area is whether the tragedy is 'disturbed' by these. You may think that it is: you may think that Aeneas's tale to Dido or the Gravedigger's riddles are an irritating distraction when tragedy is clearly brewing.

On the other hand, you will, almost certainly, not doubt the tragic impetus of the play: it begins in fear and apprehension and ends with barely a significant character still standing. Furthermore, there are many people who find the tragedy undiminished by the irrelevance and actually enhanced by the comedy. The comedy, for instance, in scenes mocking Polonius or the gravediggers scene, offers a different insight into a diseased world, as well as building tension as the audience wonders when it will turn to violence or death. There is no reason to believe that Shakespeare tried to follow the Three Unities of Classical tragedy (time, place and action), though, in fact, *Hamlet* comes nearer to fulfilling them than several of his other tragedies: *King Lear* or *Antony and Cleopatra*, for instance.

The main justification for the apparently irrelevant scenes comes in the character of Hamlet. The Prince dominates the play (it is, famously, the longest part in Shakespeare) and he is a most unusual tragic hero. This is not to say that he is inadequate in the role, though you will need to debate how effective he is as an avenger. He has nobility and a sense of honour, and he progresses along the traditional route from high admired station (in the reports of others, like Ophelia) to degradation, death and redemption. He is, however, a much more complex character. He does not express himself in battle, court or wooing scenes; on the other hand, he is as skilled in the theatre as the duel, philosophy preoccupies him as much as politics, he is at ease with fellow students and humble workers, etc. Perhaps you may conclude that the play is very much a reflection of its protagonist and his complexity of character and range of talents and interests. This is, however, an essay where the conclusion must reflect your own opinion.

■ How to write an examination essay

Preparation

- The first essential is thorough revision. You may be answering questions in either a traditional examination or an Open Book examination. It is vital that you remember that in an Open Book examination you have enough time to look up quotations and references, but only if you know where to look.

- The revision process should begin well before the examination: a matter of months rather than weeks. Initially you need to re-read texts, which is not a good idea the week before the examination. It is then useful to make notes, both to assist memory at the time and to provide a summary for later revision. These notes should be arranged to give a pattern to your study: by themes, characters, techniques, etc. Quotations should not be learned simply by rote, but together with relevant uses for them. A late stage of revision should be to fix the patterns of knowledge in your mind, probably by writing practice essays.

- The time process is very important – trying to absorb new material the night before the examination is likely to be positively harmful.

Before you start writing

- Read the questions very carefully, both to choose the most suitable title and to be certain of exactly what you are asked to do. It is very easy, but potentially disastrous, to answer the essay you *hope or imagine* has been asked, or to reproduce a practice essay you wrote on a vaguely similar theme.

- A Level questions need careful attention. Do not respond instantly to a quotation without checking what the question asks you to write about it. Make certain that you are aware of every part of a question: many ask you to do two or three distinct things, and omitting one of these immediately reduces your possible marks. Check for words like compare, contrast, analyse, consider and discuss.

- You do not have much spare time in an examination, but it is worthwhile spending a few minutes noting down the material you think is relevant, matching it with the instructions you have been given and drawing up an essay plan. Starting on the wrong essay or starting the right one in the wrong way ultimately wastes time.

- Make sure that your plan develops a consistent argument or point of view – you will not be asked to tell the story, and essays that take a chronological approach seldom do well.

Writing the essay

- The first sentences are very important. You should begin the essay by informing the examiner of the opinion you are going to develop, the contrasts you are going to study, or your view of the problem you are about to analyse. This should stay in focus throughout the essay – if possible, each paragraph should begin with a *topic sentence* relating the material of that paragraph to your overall theme or argument.

- Do not spend too long introducing the essay: move quickly to the material you wish to cover. Throughout, check your plan to make sure that you deal with all the points you wish to make.

- Quotation is particularly relevant where the style of expression is important in itself or in revealing character or the author's viewpoint. It is less important when you are referring to events. Quotations should be kept fairly short and should be relevant, not simply attractive or well known. In many cases it is possible to absorb a quotation into your sentence, but quotations of a few lines must be set out separately and as in the text.

- There is no 'correct' length for an essay. The fact that someone else is clearly writing huge amounts does not mean that he or she will obtain better marks than you. However, you should make sure that you use your time fully, write concisely and avoid padding.

- It is dangerous to exceed the allotted time for each question by more than a few minutes, especially as marks can always be gained most easily at the start of an essay. Make sure that you tackle the required number of questions. For this reason, though an elegant conclusion is desirable, it may sometimes be necessary to omit it.

- Examiners understand that candidates are writing under pressure, but it is still important that you maintain as high a standard of written expression as possible. Avoid slang, colloquialisms and contractions (e.g. 'they've' for 'they have') wherever possible.

Examination questions inevitably invite the candidate to present an argument. Decide on your position and make sure that you refer to both sides of the argument. Whether the question pertains to a theme or a specific scene in the text, you must demonstrate your knowledge of the whole text. Make sure that you refer to specific examples throughout the play in your argument.

An *outline* of a model answer has been supplied for each essay title below. Use this outline in conjunction with material in the **Who's who**, **Themes and images** and **Text commentary** sections of this guide. In addition, the points raised as **Examiner's tips** throughout the **Text commentary** should prove particularly useful.

1 *What does the theme of revenge contribute to the success of the play?*

(*NEAB*, A Level, Paper 1, 1995)

- This is a very popular subject and can be asked in this way (theme-related) or in a character-related way, comparing Hamlet's effectiveness as an avenger with Laertes' and Fortinbras's.

- It is probably wise to start with the most basic, yet most important, contribution of the theme of revenge: it makes the drama possible. You might speculate on what sort of conflict might have arisen between Hamlet and Claudius if there had been no ghost, but this particular drama derives from the moment when the Ghost says, 'Revenge his foul and most unnatural murder.' You then need to show how the plot derives from the stratagems and shifts of power that mark Hamlet's quest for revenge and Claudius's response to it.

- It is always wise not to dismiss the element of plot in a Shakespeare play. Of course you must comment on themes and characters, and simply telling the story is not an option, but *understanding* how Shakespeare tells the story is important. Revenge drives the plot and you could make a case for Hamlet's revenge being made possible only by Laertes' quest for his own vengeance. (How would Hamlet have acted without the prompt of the duel?)

- Revenge contributes a great deal to the patterning of characters. Hamlet is a character of such variety that Shakespeare provides analogues for him, characters who reflect his attitude or background in one aspect only. Laertes and Fortinbras, the avenging sons, are the most striking of these analogues, with Pyrrhus another avenger brought in briefly.

- The conventional view is that Laertes and Fortinbras provide a contrast to Hamlet as sons who do not delay over the pursuit of revenge; by implication, if Hamlet had been like them, he would have fulfilled his destiny much more effectively. However, it is nowhere near as simple as that. What does Laertes achieve by his all-or-nothing drive for revenge? Fortinbras, the determined avenger, is persuaded by Claudius to use his belligerence in a different cause and, indirectly, gains a throne by it. And who would suggest that Pyrrhus is presented as a role model? Hamlet is moved by the Player, not by Pyrrhus's revenge. It is, of course, true that Fortinbras's unthinking militarism prompts thoughts of action in Hamlet.

- You can therefore develop at length the contributions of revenge to the plot and to our understanding of Hamlet's character. The theme, however, also leads into other themes of the play. What do the avengers tell us about honour? Look at Laertes. What about the central place of family? Is the call for revenge a sacred trust for a son? It throws up contrasts of thought and action: should the avenger fly to his revenge, killing 'swoopstake' one and all, and does thought breed cowardice?

- It is always preferable to drive an essay towards a final point that follows logically but is a new consideration, not just a summary. In this case you could lead up to *Hamlet* as a variant on the revenge tragedy (also a possible opening) or to the point that Hamlet's variety and interest as a character derives in part from the gulf between his natural inclinations and the role (revenger) he is forced to play.

2 *"Those who betray Hamlet also betray themselves." Discuss.*

(*NEAB*, A Level, Paper 1, 1995)

- Note the format, a rather old-fashioned one, but still perfectly effective. The idea is to offer a statement which makes sense, but is not necessarily completely true. You are well advised not to dismiss the statement as rubbish when you 'discuss' it, but disagreement in certain areas is certainly accepted, and usually expected. The best organisation is to develop your essay on one response to the statement (agree or disagree) before qualifying your conclusions at the end. Alternatively, if you think the opposing case is very weak, demolishing it at the outset can work well.

- This statement can be seen as broadly correct, but it is subtler than you might think. There are two forms of betrayal: the practical betrayal (Rosencrantz and Guildenstern, old friends, try to take him to his death) and the emotional betrayal or the betrayal into dishonour (the Queen never tries to harm him, but it is her betrayal that hurts him most). If you consider these and the betrayal of Hamlet and the betrayal of self, there are four elements of betrayal.

- Good evidence of agreement with the statement abounds. Rosencrantz and Guildenstern are betrayed into a suitably devious death. The practical betrayals of Claudius and Laertes in Acts 4 and 5 rebound perfectly on them. Hamlet is well aware of the justice of such events, as in his comment on Rosencrantz and Guildenstern about the 'enginer' and the petard.

- If we take emotional betrayals, Gertrude, while probably not guilty of a crime as such, betrays herself into dishonour and Hamlet drives her to despair by confronting her with it. Ophelia, similarly, betraying their love, finds herself betrayed into a madness based on laments for lost love. Ophelia, of course, is part of Polonius's schemes of betrayal but, with her as with his mother, the betrayal is felt by Hamlet more as a relationship destroyed.

- This is not a difficult essay in many ways because it is possible to move from character to character, demonstrating the form the betrayals take. You could also claim that the only major character to survive at the end is the only one who never betrays Hamlet or himself: Horatio.

- Perhaps the only real doubt is whether betraying themselves is the right term for what happens to Polonius and, particularly, Claudius. Do they have better natures to betray, like Gertrude, a code of honour, like Laertes, or a bond with Hamlet, like Rosencrantz and Guildenstern, or is what happens to them simply a case of poetic justice?

75

Self-test answers Act 1

Who? Why? What? How? Where? When?
1 Horatio and Marcellus, by Marcellus (1.1, line 16)
2 Old King Hamlet, a characteristic shared by the Ghost (1.2, line 242)
3 Laertes (1.2, lines 50–56)
4 Because of the coming of morning, signalled by cock-crow or fading of glow-worms.
5 Excessive drinking (1.4, lines 8–22)
6 To have nothing to do with him (1.3, lines 132–134)
7 By striking it with his partisan (spear) (1.1, line 143)
8 To university at Wittenberg (1.2, line 113)
9 To his ship to return to France (1.3, line 1 and elsewhere)
10 Shortly before the assassination of Julius Caesar (1.1, line 116–119)

Complete the quotes
1 'How weary, stale, flat and unprofitable/Seem to me all the uses of this world!' Hamlet, 1.2, lines 133–134.
2 'With mirth in funeral and with dirge in marriage.' Claudius, 1.2, line 12.
3 'A little more than kin and less than kind.' Hamlet, 1.2, line 65.
4 'This above all: to thine own self be true...' Polonius, 1.3, line 78.
5 'The time is out of joint. O cursed spite,/That ever I was born to set it right.' Hamlet, 1.5, lines 197–198.
6 'O villain, villain, smiling damned villain!' Hamlet, 1.5, line 106.
7 'Murder most foul, as in the best it is,/But this most foul, strange and unnatural.' Ghost, 1.5, lines 27–28.
8 'He may not, as unvalu'd persons do,/Carve for himself...' Laertes, 1.3, lines 19–20.
9 'like a puff'd and reckless libertine/Himself the primrose path of dalliance treads...' Ophelia, 1.3, lines 49–50.
10 'To post/With such dexterity to incestuous sheets!' Hamlet, 1.2, lines 156–157.

Prove it!
1 There are many references to it in 1.2, including 'I doubt some foul play' (line 256), plus the use of 'prophetic' in his reaction to his uncle's crime (1.5, line 41).
2 There is much evidence in the first scene, mostly sparked by Marcellus's question (lines 73 onwards) about the manufacture of cannons and overtime for shipwrights.
3 His deference to the King in 1.2, his love of pompous moral speech and his distrust of other people in 1.3.
4 In 1.2 his refusal to let him go back to Wittenberg, determination to flatter him (e.g. lines 87/121) and his offer of a high place at Court, line 117.

Signs and themes
These are some of the examples you might choose:
Drunkenness is hinted at in 1.2, lines 125–128, and dealt with in detail in 1.4. It is a traditional failing of Danes and Hamlet is again out of step with the court.
Corruption is all around the court, with sexual corruption as strong as political. This is particularly emphasised in Hamlet's soliloquy in 1.2 and the Ghost's speeches in 1.5.
Deception is presented as something foreign to Hamlet ('I know not seems' – 1.2,

line 76), but is common to the court and the Polonius family. The extent of deception in the King is brought out by the Ghost (1.5). Finally Hamlet adopts deception: 'antic disposition' (1.5, line 180).

◼ Self-test answers Act 2

Who? Why? What? How? Where? When?
1 Reynaldo (2.1)
2 The King of Troy, his wife and a Greek warrior who killed him (2.2, line 446 onwards)
3 Rosencrantz (2.2, line 244) (not Hamlet, who says Denmark is a prison)
4 To find out what is wrong with Hamlet (2.2, lines 10–18), officially so it can be remedied, in reality so it can be suppressed
5 Because of the popularity of the child actors (2.2, line 330 onwards)
6 The tiger (2.2, line 446)
7 'Beautified' (2.2, line 111)
8 Much better than they deserve (2.2, line 524)
9 In her closet (2.1, line 77), as is the Queen in her scene with him in Act 3.
10 Never (2.2, lines 153–156)

Complete the quotes
1 'That he is mad 'tis true; 'tis true 'tis pity;/And pity 'tis 'tis true.' Polonius, 2.2, lines 97–98.
2 'And then, sir, does a this – a does – what was I about to say?' Polonius, 2.1, lines 50–51.
3 'As if he had been loosed out of hell/To speak of horrors, he comes before me.' Ophelia, 2.1, lines 83–84.
4 'What piece of work is a man, how noble in reason, how infinite in faculties...' Hamlet, 2.2, lines 303–304.
5 'What's Hecuba to him, or he to her,/That he should weep for her?' Hamlet, 2.2, lines 553–554.
6 'Happy in that we are not over-happy.' Guildenstern, 2.2, line 228.
7 'Conception is a blessing, but as your daughter may conceive – friend, look to't.' Hamlet, 2.2, lines 184–186.
8 'Your bait of falsehood takes this carp of truth.' Polonius, 2.1, line 63.
9 'Though this be madness, yet there is method in't.' Polonius, 2.2, lines 205–206.
10 'let them be well used, for they are the abstract and brief chronicles of the time.' Hamlet, 2.2, lines 519–520.

The theme of madness
1 Visiting Ophelia in her closet, with pale face, disordered clothing, etc., seizing her by the wrist, staring at her, sighing, etc. (2.1, line 77 onwards)
2 'The very ecstasy of love' (2.1, line 102)/Ophelia's rejection of him (line 110)
3 Sadness, starving himself (fast), sleeplessness (watch), weakness, wandering in his mind (lightness) and madness (2.2, lines 147–151)
4 Madness, but with some sense ('method') in it (2.2, lines 205–206)
5 Distaste for the world ('lost all my mirth') for some unknown reason (2.2, line 295 onwards); 'mad north-north-west' (line 374)
6 The take-over of the child actors; Claudius being King of Denmark (2.2, lines 359–360)
7 The Player in the Hecuba speech (2.2, line 549)

The theatre
1 Roscius (2.2, lines 385–386)
2 Seneca for tragedy; Plautus for comedy (2.2, lines 396–397)
3 The section (from 2.2, line 336) about the 'eyrie of children'.
4 The sign of the Globe (Hercules' load) (2.2, line 358)
5 Greeting the actor ('your ladyship') with comments about getting taller and voice breaking (2.2, lines 420–425)

◼ Self-test answers Act 3

Who? Why? What? How? Where? When?
1 The King, according to Guildenstern (3.2, line 293)
2 Because the King would go to heaven (3.3, line 74 onwards)
3 The Prologue to the play (3.2, line 149)
4 Not in love; not mad (3.1, lines 164–166)
5 'The dread of something after death' (3.1, line 78)
6 'To whet thy almost blunted purpose' (3.4, line 111)
7 A cloud (3.3, line 371): it also resembles a camel and a whale!
8 A nunnery (many references)
9 Behind an arras (3.4, line 6 stage direction)
10 When Lucianus pours the poison in the King's ear (3.2, line 254 stage direction, and line 259)

Complete the quotes
1 'Almost as bad, good mother,/As kill a king and marry with his brother.' Hamlet (3.4, lines 28–29)
2 ''Sblood, do you think I am easier to be played on than a pipe?' Hamlet (3.2, lines 360–361)
3 'To die, to sleep;/To sleep, perchance to dream – ay, there's the rub.' Hamlet (3.1, lines 64–65)
4 'Th'observed of all observers, quite, quite down!' Ophelia (3.1, line 156)
5 'O, my offence is rank, it smells to heaven;/It hath the primal eldest curse upon't – /A brother's murder.' Claudius (3.3, lines 36–38)
6 'Thou turn'st my eyes into my very soul.' Gertrude (3.4, line 89)
7 'It was a brute part of him to kill so capital a calf there.' Hamlet (3.2, lines 104–105)
8 'There's something in his soul/O'er which his melancholy sits on brood.' Claudius (3.1, lines 166–167)
9 'My words fly up, my thoughts remain below.' Claudius (3.3, line 97)
10 'You are the Queen, your husband's brother's wife,/And, would it were not so, you are my mother.' Hamlet (3.4, lines 14–15)

The pangs of conscience
1 Both conscience and the power of thought persuade us to be cowards, not take action, as in suicide.
2 'None wed the second but who kill'd the first' in the play. This is likely to stir Gertrude's conscience, though the suggestion is not that she killed her husband – the two crimes of murder and marriage are seen as one by Hamlet and she automatically becomes an accomplice.
3 Because his thoughts remain below. His sense of guilt is real, but he is not willing to part with what he gained by murder.

4 Her response goes from haughty dismissal, to silence, to pleas for him to stop, to a heart 'cleft in twain'.

5 To make him fulfil his oath a) to gain revenge and b) to spare his mother.

Sexual disgust

There are far too many examples to list, but the best quotations can be found:

- in the beauty/honesty/calumny images, plus the scathing description of painted women and the two meanings of 'nunnery' – 3.1;
- in the suggestive conversation with Ophelia before the play – 3.2;
- in his tormenting Gertrude's conscience at the play – 3.2 – and, more strongly, in her closet – 3.4;
- in the tortured descriptions of Claudius and Gertrude in bed – 3.4.

◼ Self-test answers Acts 4 and 5

Who? Why? What? How? Where? When?

1 Osric (5.2)

2 A Norman who praised Laertes' skill with the rapier when he visited the Danish Court (4.7, line 80 onwards)

3 Osric describes Laertes (5.2, lines 107–108)

4 Because of Ophelia's reduced funeral obsequies (5.1, lines 233–235)

5 Claudius is no longer alive; he did not want the King of England to kill Rosencrantz and Guildenstern (5.2, lines 377–379)

6 Old Hamlet defeated old Fortinbras and the Gravedigger started work (5.1, lines 139–144)

7 'they withered all when my father died.' (4.5, lines 182–183)

8 By means of a letter delivered by sailors (4.6)

9 'Th'other place' (Hell) (4.3, lines 33–35)

10 After Hamlet has won two bouts at fencing (5.2, line 295 stage direction)

Complete the quotes

1 'There is a willow grows aslant the brook/That shows his hoary leaves in the glassy stream.' Gertrude, 4.7, lines 165–166.

2 'But I cannot choose but weep to think they would lay him i'th' cold ground.' Ophelia, 4.5, lines 68–70.

3 'For he was likely, had he been put on,/To have prov'd most royal.' Fortinbras, 5.2, lines 402–403.

4 'I am more an antique Roman than a Dane.' Horatio, 5.2, line 346.

5 'I knew him, Horatio, a fellow of infinite jest, of most excellent fancy.' Hamlet, 5.1, lines 178–179.

6 'Imperious Caesar, dead and turn'd to clay,/Might stop a hole to keep the wind away.' Hamlet, 5.1, lines 206–207.

7 'I thought thy bride-bed to have deck'd, sweet maid,/And not have strew'd thy grave.' Gertrude, 5.1, lines 238–239.

8 'Do it, England:/For like the hectic in my blood he rages,/And thou must cure me.' Claudius, 4.3, lines 68–70.

9 'Now get you to my lady's chamber and tell her, let her paint an inch thick, to this favour she must come.' Hamlet, 5.1, lines 186–188.

10 'But I do prophesy th'election lights/On Fortinbras.' Hamlet, 5.2, lines 360–361.

The fact of death

The following lists are by no means complete, but suggest the sort of references you should have found.

1 Decay (worm and smell references) and the pointlessness of our mortal pride and dignity: 'a king may go a progress through the guts of a beggar' (lines 30–31)

2 The heroism (or folly) of sacrificing 'two thousand souls' (line 25) for a piece of land not worth five ducats (line 20)

3 Many songs dwell on the sense of loss and the death of innocence: e.g. 'He is dead and gone, lady' (line 29)

4 Innocence lost and pathetic charm: '…from her melodious lay/To muddy death.' (lines 181–182)

5 The power of the grave: the gravedigger is the strongest builder (lines 57–59). Macabre comedy and lack of reverence (as in songs)

6 Much about decay (e.g. the discussion of tanners – line 162 onwards) and the transience of earthly dignity and glory, as in 4.3 (e.g. many references to who the skulls may have belonged to or the Caesar rhyme – line 206 onwards)

7 Like Rosencrantz and Guildenstern each is 'hoist with his own petard' (3.4). Compare Laertes' 'The foul practice/Hath turn'd itself on me.' (lines 323–324).

8 Acceptance of Fate, but needs Horatio to 'report me and my cause aright' (line 344)

Extras

Many of these have a specific role, especially as messengers (e.g. the sailors), whether or not specified as ''Messenger'. Many events in the last two acts happen off stage, notably the fight with the pirates, the death of Ophelia, the return of Hamlet and the deaths of Rosencrantz and Guildenstern, and therefore these must be reported. The speech about Laertes (4.5, line 98 onwards) is a particularly fine 'Messenger' speech.

The absence of Polonius, Rosencrantz and Guildenstern creates a need for courtiers, like the Gentleman: even Horatio plays this role briefly.

Fortinbras, of course, is a key element in the trio of avenging sons and the Captain assists in giving information that reinforces his contrast with Hamlet. Fortinbras also is an essential component in the restoration of normality.

The Gravediggers and Osric preserve the delicate balance between tragedy and comedy in the absence of characters who previously were targets for Hamlet's humour. In addition to playing important roles connected with Ophelia's funeral and the final duel, the Gravedigger maintains the theme of macabre comedy (plus serious comments on the transience of life) and Osric's affectation provides a new target for Hamlet's sardonic attacks on society and Court manners.